No More Work Days:

The Journey to Making

Every Day a Saturday

By

Sam Crowley

NO MORE WORK DAYS:

The Journey to Making

EVERY DAY A SATURDAY

DEDICATION

This book is dedicated to my beautiful wife Angela, who has stuck by me for the past 17 years, through all the ups and downs and all the crazy ideas you will read about in this book. She thought she married a corporate executive and was in for a nice, secure life. Little did she know that she actually locked herself into the front seat of a never-ending roller coaster.

To my daughters, Madeline, Laura and Paige: You are the reason I do what I do. I would never have had the motivation to go for my dream, had you not entered the world. Each day I think of how lucky I am to be your father.

To my mother, Catherine Crowley (1927-1997): You raised eight kids by yourself, still the most amazing accomplishment I have ever witnessed. Thank you for giving me the gift of life, a sharp wit and the permission to use my voice.

To all my brothers and sisters: Chris, Kate, Richard, Justin, Sooz, Bernie and Jim. Elm Street in Bradford, PA is gone but the great memories are still clear in my mind. You've all played a role in raising me when mom couldn't always be there. Thank you.

CONTENTS

INTRODUCTION

"Who's Sam Crowley?"

Good question – and one that was weaving its way inexorably around each and every grouping of lounge chairs poolside at the Hilton Hawaiian Village in Waikiki. Actually, it was more like, "I see the first speaker on the conference agenda is Lee Brower. I've read his chapter on gratitude in The Secret. But then we've got...Sam Crowley? Who the hell is Sam Crowley? I've never heard of him – have you?"

I have to admit I was shamelessly eavesdropping while stretched out on a deck chair, soaking up the Hawaiian sun and pretending to read the newspaper. I didn't really want to hear the comments of the myriad conference attendees surrounding my deck chair, all of them easily identified by the lanyard with the company logo of the conference sponsor swinging about their necks, but it was impossible not to pay attention.

Of course they didn't know me! Not only was tomorrow's speech going to be my first ever paid engagement, heck, it was only the second time I'd flown in my life. Listening to the comments of all these people expecting to be informed and entertained by me – me, Sam Crowley, the nobody – tomorrow was making my palms sweat.

Who was Sam Crowley, indeed, and how did I get here? That was the question I needed to answer tomorrow, publicly, in front of a huge audience. I was expected to speak for four hours and the PowerPoint I'd put together over the last two weeks wouldn't fill even half that time. It would mark the culmination of everything I'd been striving for over the last several years.

I folded up my newspaper, slid my feet into a pair of flip flops, and slipped away from the pool deck to head for my room.

By the time the great orange ball of a sun dipped below the silhouettes of pineapple and palm trees, I was lying between silky linen hotel sheets but still wide awake. After tossing and turning for hours in the unfamiliar hotel bed, I finally got up and padded out onto the small patio overlooking the Pacific Ocean. I breathed in the air, liberally scented with hibiscus and sea spray. Tomorrow everything changes.

The hours up until the conference passed at a snail's pace. Even without more than a few minutes' sleep, I was wide awake and ready to go promptly at eight in the morning. After a splash of cool water on my face, I made my way to the green room located behind the stage in the hotel's conference center. It was less than an hour until show time, when 1,200 people would gather to hear me speak. I walked onto the stage, and parted the closed drapes to peer out at the rows of theatre seating.

So this is what it feels like to be Zig Ziglar or Les Brown or Tony Robbins. Hmm…It feels pretty good, kind of like…home.

The dialogue of excited conference attendees bounced off the walls of the venue as people began filing down the aisles and into seats. Shouts and laughter, footfalls and the rustle of paper were deadened by the acoustic material on the walls but I couldn't help but think they were still wondering, "Who the hell is Sam Crowley?"

An hour went by both faster and slower than I'd ever thought possible. While I paced around backstage, the event's host made his entrance and warmed up the crowd. After a couple minutes' worth of bad jokes, he introduced me, "You're in for a real treat today. We've got Sam Crowley, who runs Every Day is Saturday. Sam started the company because every day he worked his corporate job his young daughter ask him if tomorrow was Saturday. Get ready to be motivated and inspired by Sam Crowley."

Finally, there was my cue. After one last silent prayer and a quick wipe of wet palms on my pants, I was more than ready to go. I didn't just walk, I ran onto the stage full of an energy that I didn't have to fake.

The crowd went wild. Even though they had no clue who I was, they were transfixed and transformed by my energetic entrance. I was on fire and so was the audience.

I glanced out over the blurry sea of faces shouting and screaming my name and thought back to the first Every Day is Saturday event I'd scheduled months earlier, when I'd asked my wife to get online with me because no one else had showed up. But this was different. These people wanted to hear my message. They were ramped up by nothing more than seeing me standing onstage – the vision of which was amplified by two huge screens on either side – and so far they loved me!

A handful of conflicting emotions threatened to overwhelm me. Now that I was here, onstage in Hawaii, I had to perform up to expectations. But it was so exhilarating! I already felt famous! And that was my reward for staying in the game, for doing what I didn't want to do all those long years with my nose to the corporate grindstone, for moving my family time after time in response to bad management decisions, for spending an entire week learning how to make sub sandwiches, for having to swallow my pride in order to support my family. All those bad decisions were in the past. Today was now the tomorrow when everything changed; today was finally my Saturday.

After the applause died down I fingered the clicker in my pants pocket that would advance my

PowerPoint to the first slide in my presentation. I opened my mouth and began to deliver my message...and found that I didn't need a single one of those slides I'd so painstakingly prepared. The clicker was forgotten as I told stories and jokes and laughed along the way. The words flowed and the audience responded positively, laughing at my hilarities and groaning in shared misery at the stories of unhappy, backstabbing coworkers I'd put up with for the majority of my career.

Those first two hours of my presentation seemed like mere minutes. The first intermission came at eleven o'clock. While the crowd was still applauding I slipped backstage, where an event worker asked if she could iron my shirt. The owner of the sponsor company who'd hired me for the conference met me in the green room with a hearty handshake and a broad smile. "You are amazing! Where have you been hiding? Why haven't we had you at one of our events before?"

Little did he know that just six months earlier I'd been shoveling snow off the sidewalk in front of my rental properties in Bradford, Pennsylvania, blowing on my fingers to keep them from cramping due to extreme cold. And now? I was in Hawaii!

While the lady ironing my shirt asked if she could do anything else for me, the owner gave me a thumbs up on his way back to his front row seat and told me to keep on "crushing it." Since his company had contracted my services for $25,000 as well as reimbursing my travel expenses, I figured it was the least I could do to get back out there and "crush it", indeed.

When I bounded back onstage after the 15 minute intermission, I was still winging my presentation, having completely abandoned the PowerPoint. I decided to bring several members of the audience up on stage with me and ask them to paint a picture of their Saturday, which resulted in hundreds of attendees vying to join in the fun. Even though I was on a roll, the night was coming to a close as I finished my last segment with a handful of motivational teaching stories.

"It has been an unbelievable journey for me to be here with you today. The good news is that you get to take a piece of me with you when you leave. But what's even better is that I get to take a piece of you with me when I leave. See you later, Champions!" I waved as I walked off stage. The crowd went nuts.

This time when I heard my name, it was the chanting of a ramped up group of over a 1,000 people all screaming to hear more instead of wondering who the hell I was! I actually had to be escorted out of the conference hall through the kitchen because so many of those who'd heard my message vied for my attention, pushing forward and shouting my name, wanting nothing more than to continue hearing what I had to say.

I had another two days to spend in Hawaii. Where before I'd lounged around the pool in anonymity, after that presentation I couldn't step foot on the elevator without hearing an excited cry of "Hey, Champion!" I was accosted when I stepped into the restaurant each morning to get a cup of coffee and stopped by eager fans on my way to the pool.

The night after the event, I attended a traditional luau for the conference attendants at the hotel. Little did I know that famous speakers rarely show up at events like this. But since I wasn't famous yet and this was all new to me, I decided to attend, along with a thousand conference attendees still proudly sporting their corporate lanyards. I barely got one foot through the door before cameras started flashing, people were thrusting babies into my arms for family photo ops, and programs were shoved into my hand for me to add my autograph.

Every time I turned around, someone was offering me a drink and asking if I needed anything.

My wife Angela's face flashed in my mind's eye. I could just picture her rolling her eyes over all this attention and reminding me, "You're just Sam, ordinary Sam." Not today, sweetheart, I'm Sam, the Motivational Speaker! Ha! There was an extra spring in my step as I headed for the door.

Even though I hadn't slept for two days, I couldn't seem to break free of the throngs of people still contending for my attention. I left the bar that night after the luau and a hundred or so of them followed me to my room. They didn't want me to leave; in fact they chased me down the hallway amid roars of "Champion!" When the elevator dinged at my floor I had to run out of the car in order to escape!

When I finally laid down to get some much-needed rest, my mind was still racing. I pulled out the check I'd received from my company contact at the luau, my eyes darting across the line that read "Pay to the order of Sam Crowley" right above the one that read, "$12,500". I was finally able to absorb that it was me who'd wowed the crowd in Waikiki, me who was showered with accolades, me who was asked to return and deliver yet another motivational and inspiring speech.

Before I departed the hotel for the airport I checked in with my conference contact one last time. I practically floated out the door when she told me, "Sam, you are the best speaker we've ever had at one of our conferences." Really? Me?

The truth was I could still hardly believe that I'd finally made it to my Saturday. Not only that, I'd been able to share my message with others and let them know it's possible for anyone – even an ordinary Joe like me – to find success and achieve the life goals you so truly desire, whatever they may be.

You've heard stories about how people have been in the right place at the right time and gotten discovered by an agent to later become rich and famous. I'm here to tell you, agents are not required. I went from nobody special to somebody others admired simply by discovering myself; discovering what it is that really makes me tick. This wasn't a fluke; I'd worked hard and long to get here and let me say, what a long, strange trip it's been!

I'm Sam Crowley. And this is my story of starting out life just like you, in an ordinary way with an ordinary life. Somewhere along the way I got enough guts and motivation and stick-to-it-iveness to start my own business doing something that's enjoyable, something that doesn't seem like work at all.

This is your chance to get out of the Monday to Friday grind once and for all and make every day of your life the Saturday you now look forward to all week long, just like I did. Come with me and see what I'm talking about. You just might discover something new and important about yourself along the way.

Are you ready, Champion?

CHAPTER ONE:

I GET BORED EASILY

You know that song from the musical, Annie, "The Sun Will Come Up Tomorrow"? Yeah, I hate it, too. But hearing that red-headed tyke singing at the top of her little lungs reminds me that no matter what stupid things I do today, tomorrow is another day.

I've always been one to not only push the envelope, but to send it hurtling into deep space. I believe there are no rules in life and if someone tries to convince you there are, well, they're full of it. If you fail, you fail. So what? The sun will come up tomorrow and you'll have another chance to make a fool of yourself all over again. But that's the beauty of a life without rules.

Back when I was just starting my first career, in my early twenties, I liked to refer to myself as "psychologically unemployable." That was largely because of that no rules style of living I embraced. My hero was Michael J. Fox in *The Secret of My Success*. If you haven't seen that movie (and chances are you haven't if you're not over the age of 40), it's about a college graduate from Kansas who moves to New York City for a job as a financier. He gets fired due to a corporate takeover and takes a job at another firm as a mailroom clerk. When a cushy corner office becomes vacant, Fox takes it over, convincing everyone he's a newly hired executive. Of course, just as you'd expect from Hollywood, he goes on to save the company from financial ruin and gets the girl (the CEO's daughter). Just like Michael J. Fox's character, I didn't want to work my way up the corporate ladder the long, hard way; I wanted to scurry up as fast as I could go without regard for anything standing in my way.

I first realized my incredible level of boredom when I was in college, at the start of my sophomore year at Pennsylvania State's Erie campus. I was sitting in a philosophy class wondering what I would ever use philosophy for in the real world. For that matter, when would I ever use any of the "knowledge" I'd learned in any of my classes? This wasn't real life; real life in all its no-holds-barred glory was waiting for me somewhere down the road but it would never visit the classroom at Penn State. I was bored out of my mind with academia.

This was the first time boredom would cause me to make a rash decision – but certainly not the last!

After Christmas break of my sophomore year I decided I just didn't want to go to class anymore. I'd much rather hang out and do something fun. Of course, it wasn't my money I was wasting. As the youngest of eight kids from an impoverished family, I'd gotten a free ride to Penn State via a government-sponsored Pell grant.

It didn't help matters that my dorm mate made the lead character in the movie *Dude, Where's My Car?* look like a rocket scientist. Upon moving into the dorm, my first interaction with the guy was a quick introduction followed by his description of college life as, "A never-ending party with a $30,000 cover charge." With my track record of breaking rules as fast as they could be made, I needed to be in a monastery rooming with a guy wearing a pocket protector, not cohabitating with Mr. Party Animal.

Even with a constant barrage of parties during my first year and a half of college, I managed to stay mildly focused on my studies. Of course, it didn't hurt that I'd opted to drop any remotely difficult courses and stick with mostly gym and health classes in order to carry a full load and keep my grant.

A week before the semester ended in the middle of my sophomore year, I called my mom and told her I was going to drop out. At that time no one had yet realized that I wasn't showing up in class due to boredom and I guess I just needed to confide in someone. My mom, bless her heart, was shocked that I could even consider throwing away such a wonderful opportunity. "I'm going to join the army," was my response to her question of what I was going to do with myself. But since I can't stand taking orders, that wasn't going to work out so well. What the heck, that was just an inconsequential detail.

Without a clue as to where I was headed in life, I went ahead with my plan to drop out – but I waited until May so my academic record would reflect a series of incompletes rather than failing grades. In order to make my defection official, I had to visit the Admissions Office before noon. In order to get there, I had to pass by the front of a big campus building where the majority of classes were held and many of my party buddies were loitering. It felt like the Bataan death march. I kept my eyes glued to the sidewalk and pulled my hoodie up over my eyebrows, striving for anonymity, but it didn't work. As I walked by, I was greeted by a chorus of yells. "Crowley! Man, what are you doing here? It's noon – why aren't you still in bed?" All I wanted to do was sign the paperwork to drop out of college and then be on my way, but everyone I knew was there to witness my shame.

Because I'd already told my mom I was going to enlist, that's what I did. I know, it was a dumb move, another one of those bad decisions brought about by extreme boredom and a desire to not move back into my mom's house and drain the rest of her meager finances. In June of 1988 I walked into my local recruiter's office in Bradford, Pennsylvania. Filled with promises of an education that would get me into a lucrative career later, I signed the papers committing my body and soul to the United States Army for the next four years.

This was going to be a piece of cake! I like playing the game *Clue* and watching crime dramas so I thought I'd shoot for a position within the FBI. I would start by majoring in accounting because in those days, in order to join the storied ranks of the Federal Bureau of Investigation, you had to be either an accountant or a lawyer. I didn't figure I was cut out to be a lawyer so that made my choice pretty clear.

The aptitude tests required for enlistment were being given in Pittsburgh so I hopped on the bus along with an entire batch of new recruits. The United States Army put us up in a cheap motel the night before testing. With nothing better to do, the lot of us decided to go drinking. It was like college all over again, being paired with Mr. Party Animal for a roomie. I really couldn't hang with this crowd and expect anything good to come of it but I'd already taken the sworn oath and gotten my picture snapped in front of the American flag. I couldn't get out of this one...

The next day I was lined up with the rest of the recruits nursing a pounding headache and a cotton-filled mouth. Because I could barely stand without barfing, I propped myself against the wall with the help of one foot. Along comes a ranking officer to inspect our sorry asses. Of course he noticed me right away, "Crowley! Get your foot off the wall. We stand at attention in the army!"

My flippant response? "I'm not in the army yet!"

The officer proceeded to ask me where I was going to be stationed and I told him Fort Jackson. He let me know he'd make sure they took care of me there. Not even a day in the service and I already had a target on my back!

The next hurdle to jump for enlistment was a background check and interview to ensure that I was mentally ready to function in a military intelligence capacity.

By this time I was pretty sure I made a huge mistake. What was I thinking? I can't take orders! I was already bored with the entire enlistment process; I couldn't imagine actually going through basic training.

I sat in a sterile little room with the interviewer, who was determined to draw out all my deep, dark secrets. "I see you went to college for the last two years. How many beers did you have?" I thought about it for a few seconds. I didn't want to give him a ridiculous answer so I just told him I had no idea. He persisted, "Give me a guess." Did this guy realize I had to count in kegs, not bottles? Every Friday night my dorm roomies and I bought 25 cases of beer to host the biggest parties on campus– and that was a low week.

I asked him why he wanted to know. "We don't want drunks in the army." As he continued questioning me, an idea began to form. Maybe for once telling the truth would be the best option.

"All right, Sam. I'm going to describe a situation and I want you to imagine what you'd do. Okay? Let's say you were working undercover and you were sent into a bar. A Russian KGB agent spots you in the bar and presses you for information. Would you continue drinking? Now I want you to answer honestly because when you're in military intelligence, you're in. There's no backing out."

I pretended to think long and hard about my answer. I could hear the waiting music from Jeopardy playing in my head while I waited just long enough to make the interviewer think I was giving his question serious consideration. Finally I answered, "Hmm, that's a tough one but I gotta tell you, if I'm drunk, I'm giving all the information I have to the Russian KGB officer. That's my honest answer." I shrugged, as if to say, "Hey, I'm not perfect."

The interviewer frowned and excused himself to call my answers into Quantico. Even though he closed the door, I could hear everything that was going on. The guy didn't need to call Quantico, D.C. or even Duluth. He waited outside the door for a few minutes, then strode back in with his official military non-expression firmly in place. "I'm sorry, Sam, but you're not ready for military intelligence at this time. However, if you work hard the next couple years, we'll reevaluate your readiness. In the meantime, you can be a food specialist or a cargo specialist. How does that sound?"

You mean I can cook or sling boxes onto a dock? "If I don't sign, I don't have to go into the army, right?"

That took the interviewer aback. "Well, technically, yes. But you have to give back your signing bonus."

"Thanks for the opportunity, but no thanks." I ran out of that interviewer's office so fast, the papers on his desk fluttered in the breeze. By the time I got home I'd received several calls from my recruiter, which I didn't return.

I'd just learned how to use an escape clause. I'd also just realized I need to be more judicious about taking risks and not being too stupid.

However, I was still bored and I still didn't have any idea what I was going to do with my life. College was now out of the question and so was enlisting in the army. I continued to look for an instant injection of excitement. I wasn't finding it in any of the bars in Bradford, PA but that didn't stop me from being a frequent customer.

I met a buddy at the Option House bar one night at the end of that summer in 1988. By the time the bar was closing at two a.m. and the alcohol had been flowing all night, he asked me what I was going to do with my life. His plan was to drive to West Palm Beach in the next couple days in order to attend college. So, recognizing the opportunity when I saw it, I asked him if I could ride along. He asked me if I'd ever been to Florida. "Nope. The furthest south I've ever been is Washington, D.C. It's a 23-hour drive? I'm in!" Once again, the fact that I get bored easily was the key factor in what I decided to do with my life.

In August of '88, my buddy and I piled into his Pontiac Grand Prix and headed south for sunny Florida. We found a cheap duplex to rent, although we didn't have any way to furnish it. No bed to sleep in? No problem. I went dumpster diving and found a perfectly good, albeit stained, mattress that I confiscated and hauled up the stairs into the apartment and into my bedroom.

While my roommate went to school each day, I went through the local newspaper perusing the classified ads. There were plenty of jobs available if one wasn't too particular.

One of the first ads I saw was for a clerk at a pet store. I called the place and got an interview. When I walked through the door that afternoon, the proprietor didn't bother with a lot of unnecessary questions; he just asked me if I could start right away. *Uh, no, let me check my schedule – I'm booked for the next several months...* "Sure."

So it wasn't my dream job. I figured that maybe I could work my way up the chain of command and eventually take over the cushy job of managing the place and telling someone else what to do.

It was just before closing and the owner of the pet store asked me to move a half dozen rabbits up to the front window display so people walking by could see the cute bunnies and return in the morning to buy one. I wasn't given any direction in how to do this but I figured, hey, how hard could it be to move a few bunnies across the store? They were cute and small and furry – completely innocent. I reached my hand into the cage and grabbed a few of them.

If you've never wrangled rabbits before, don't believe what you see in cartoons. They are not soft little bundles of fur; they are vicious killers! Those bunnies clawed and bit and kicked and scratched me. I dropped several of them and took to transporting them two at a time from the back of the store to the display up front. By the time I was done making a handful of trips, I looked

like I'd been in a cage fight with both Rambo and
Naomi Campbell.

As I limped out of the store at seven thirty
that night, the owner cheerfully gave me a wave
and told me I'd done a great job. Two blocks from
home I called him from a pay phone and told him I
was sorry but I'd gotten another job and wouldn't
be back to the pet store; I'd had an interview and
the new place wanted me to start Monday.

"But Sam," he said. "It's Saturday night.
It's rather unusual that you got an interview at this
time of night for a job that starts Monday morning."
Did he know I was lying? Naw!

The next want ad I called on was for a job
at a menswear store in the mall. At this time, in the
late eighties, the economy was going gangbusters
and retailers were extremely busy. Once again, I
was hired on the spot. The only qualifications were
the ability to fog up a mirror and show up on time
each day.

When I'd moved to Florida with my buddy, I didn't have a lot of possessions to bring along, let alone a lot of clothes. I was the proud owner of one pair of shorts, one pair of khaki pants, a pair of docksiders shoes, a pink shirt with a white collar, and a blue shirt with a white collar (those were the days of high fashion, eh?). For this job at the menswear store, I needed to look sharp. I couldn't wear the same outfit two days in a row so I had to switch between those two shirts every day and pray the manager wouldn't notice.

The job itself was pretty easy, especially since I hadn't yet proved I could be trusted. Every morning I took the bus to work and once I arrived at the store, took inventory. I had to count the suits. That was it; counting men's suits. If a customer came in needing assistance, I was to grab another employee for help. By no means was I to try and help a customer.

Being the easily bored person I am, I'd already been looking for another job while using the menswear store position to scrape by. I answered another want ad; this one with a big headline: BE A STOCKBROKER! MAKE $100,000 A YEAR AND MORE!

I didn't even stop to think about what I'd need to know before I could entertain making $10 a year let alone a hundred grand. I went in for an interview, thinking I would once again charm my way into an instant job. But this time it wasn't so easy. There was a test involved. All applicants were required to take the Series 7 exam and the entirety of the applicant pool were college graduates, although only 30 percent, on average, would pass. The interviewer asked me if I'd had any kind of college background. I admitted to getting a D in Economics but assured him I was a quick learner.

There was only one catch – and it was a big one for someone in my financial circumstances.

The test cost $500 and Joe, the guy interviewing me, assured me there was a slim to none chance I would pass. But somehow I got him to agree to sponsor me. I quickly followed that by asking him to loan me the $500. "Obviously I'll make commissions for you and I can pay you back right after I get started." Although I had no idea what I was talking about, it sounded right.

I felt this was the perfect opportunity for me. My sponsor was all of 24 years old, drove a shiny black Porsche and rented a $10,000 a month apartment on South Ocean Boulevard amongst the rich and famous of South Florida. Joe was as young and just as cocky as I was; we instantly hit it off. But he wasn't a pushover. I called him every night after getting home from the menswear store hounding him to loan me the $500 for two weeks straight but he avoided all my calls. After two weeks I guess Joe was tired of being hounded and he finally took my call. I knew it was the only chance I had to afford the exam fee and somehow I sold him on the idea of lending me the money. Bingo! I was in! Series 7 exam here I come!

I had a Sony Walkman I borrowed from my buddy and a bundle of prep tapes on the stockbroker's exam that I borrowed from Joe. Every day for a month I listened to those tapes nonstop and learned how to trade securities, how to make long and short trades and more. I picked up all the vernacular necessary for brokering stocks and not some insignificant amount of knowledge.

I still had to keep my day job in order to pay my share of the bills at the duplex my buddy and I rented. The sales associates at the menswear store were all snappy dressers, especially Phillip, the store manager who was British and never seen without every hair in place and a spit shine on his shoes. The rest of them didn't have his cultured British accent but they dressed just as sharply. Then there was me – the kid in dirty, scuffed docksiders and those two shirts with white collars.

One day all the sales associates left to grab coffee at a kiosk in the mall, leaving me in the store by myself. I wasn't allowed to talk to customers but as fate would have it, just minutes after they all paraded out the door to purchase lattes and cappuccinos, in walked a customer. He was a regular, an attorney who was one of Phillip's favorite clients. I told the guy Phillip wasn't available but I'd be happy to help him. After all, I counted suits every morning, the short, medium, long and portly varieties, so I knew exactly where they were all located. I looked the attorney up and down, sizing him up. He was short and fat. "You want a suit? Let me point you in the right direction. The portly section is right over here." Unfortunately, I wasn't supposed to use that term; the portly suits were referred to as "executive cut" in front of portly customers.

Phillip returned a few minutes later and homed right in on me helping the attorney sort through our assortment of large-sized suits. His face turned white as a sheet. Phillip pulled me aside and asked me what I'd said to the man. "I asked him to follow me to the portly section, that's all." Phillip dramatically drew the back of his hand over his eyes and shuttered delicately. "No, no, no! That's 'executive cut', you imbecile!"

Needless to say, I didn't last much longer at the menswear store. I'd taken the only opportunity I'd had to speak and flubbed it big time. That's when I decided I needed to learn exactly what to say at exactly the right time. I'd do better at my next job as stockbroker; I already had the right vocabulary. Yep, I was confident I'd pass the test and start driving a Porsche along South Beach Boulevard any day – my knack for getting bored easily be damned!

Chapter Two:

The Bottom Rung of the Corporate Ladder

One thing to remember no matter who you are and what you do is that just as quick as you can gain it all, it can be lost. I think many of us found this out firsthand during the recent economic turndown which proved that no job was absolutely secure. In my case it's usually boredom that causes me to give up on one venture and start the next, but it could just as easily be other circumstances that force me to take a step back and decide the next move in the chess game of life.

I had stars in my eyes imagining what it would be like to start a career as a high-powered stock broker. As I mentioned before, back in the late eighties, everything was sunshine and roses as far as the economy was concerned. Floridians had money and they had no problem spending it, on everything from luxury beachfront condos to mounds of cocaine. Although I didn't really desire either of those things, the lifestyle was easy to envy.

After weeks of nonstop studying, I was finally ready to take the Series 7 exam to become a stockbroker with my sponsor Joe footing the bill. I drove down to Fort Lauderdale with another applicant just as anxious as I was to get that test over and done with so he could start right in on brokering. When we got there, we found the examination room filled with guys in tailored suits and Italian leather loafers. I was the youngest of the bunch, yet probably the most confident (or maybe it was cocky).

A week after the exam I got a call from Joe's company. I'd passed the exam! Wait…I did? I asked if he was sure the passing grade was right and that it was really mine. He assured me it was and told me I could start Monday. In just two short months I'd gone from moving to Florida with hardly a buck in my wallet to getting mauled by rabbits in the pet store to inventorying suits beneath Phillip's watchful eye to this…a stockbroker!

Starting a new job, even one as prestigious as stock brokering, didn't come with an advance paycheck, however. I still didn't have enough money to buy my own car and the one big meal I ate each day consisted of two slices of white bread microwaved with a piece of cheese and a bowl of white rice, washed down with iced tea made from a powdered mix. After I got my first paycheck from the brokerage, I splurged on a meal at Wendy's, which to me tasted like gourmet grub. It was the most meat and vegetables I'd had in two months.

For the next two years I worked as a stockbroker in south Florida making money and living a life I'd never dreamed of when living in Bradford PA. I was finally able to afford a car and I bought a 1976 Toyota Corolla with 225,000 miles, an AM radio as the only source of music and a stick shift for my first set of wheels. It wasn't the Porsche Joe sped around town in but it was better than being stuffed in a seat next to sweaty commuters on the bus.

It didn't take me long get into the groove of my new life as a stockbroker. I started hanging around people who easily made $30,000 to $50,000 *per month*. I was invited to the same parties they were, shindigs that took place in expansive penthouse suites lining Ocean Boulevard, filled with beautiful furnishings, both live and inanimate.

Ah, now this was the life. I was in my early twenties, a college dropout. But by hanging around the right people – those who had managed to climb their way several rungs higher up the ladder of success – I, too, could benefit. Just by hanging around the movers and shakers in the industry, I learned enough to change my life forever.

Being in the industry, I was fascinated by everything that had to do with stock brokering. When the movie *Wall Street* came out in 1987 I was still in Pennsylvania, but after starting my career as stock broker in Florida, I rented the video and watched it at the dollar matinee at least 20 times. I was absolutely mesmerized by Michael Douglas' performance as Gordon Gekko. That's who I wanted to be; I wanted that power, that money, that charisma.

Luckily, I didn't get caught in the trap of thinking I could use the same unsavory tactics portrayed in the movie to make the big bucks.

Instead, I opted to give the job my best shot. Up to this point I'd only made halfhearted attempts at achieving goals (my short two years in college comes to mind) but this opportunity was different. I would get into the office each morning at seven a.m., before my coworkers, and prepare for a long day of dialing for dollars. I made at least four hundred phone calls per day, pitching a newsletter to opt people in to our mailing list. Three weeks later a senior broker would call them back to pitch stock purchases.

The company kept a department of eight men and women on the phone all day long, every day. We worked in an area of the office called 'The Pit' designated for the employees clinging to the lowest rungs of the corporate ladder, assigned to cold call. Calls started at eight in the morning to the east coast and kept going until eight at night to west coast numbers. To keep us motivated, our supervisor would turn over a chair in the middle of the room, stand on top of it swinging a baseball bat and exhort us to "Get on the phone! Call, call, call!"

Here I was imagining myself the next Gordon Gekko when in reality I was working in nothing more than a glorified sweat shop. As one of four hundred poor souls, my job was to stay on the phone all day long so I could give qualified leads to the senior broker, who got all the actual sales.

It was quite an adrenaline rush to work in the crazy, loud, fast-paced environment of the brokerage firm. But just as always, over time I got bored. Even though I was one of the lead producers at the firm and rewarded with the ability to make free long distance phone calls, it wasn't enough to keep me motivated.

At the end of each day, index finger numb from dialing the phone, I would hit the party scene. After my Corolla conked out on the freeway one day I replaced it with a sportier Celica I leased at a 21 percent interest rate. I drove that Celica around town like it was a Maserati. I finally moved out of that run-down duplex in the ghetto, to which I'd first moved with my buddy two years earlier, but even a change of scenery didn't alleviate the monotony of my day-to-day life.. I was getting tired of the heat and I missed the change of seasons. I guess I wasn't destined to live like Sonny Crockett after all.

At the end of my second year in West Palm Beach I quit my job as stockbroker and moved back to New York, this time to Buffalo. Talk about extremes! I'd gone from a place where it was summer all year long to the upper reaches of the States, where snowfall was measured not by the inch but by the foot.

I crashed with a buddy for a while until I got a lead on a roommate opportunity with another friend's sister. She put an ad in the paper and a girl had responded but they were still looking for a third person to share the rent. Maybe they wouldn't mind having a guy in the house. With visions of turning *Three's Company* into real life, I moved in with the two girls in February.

It just made sense that I would then get a job as a bartender – what else does a guy living with two girls do for a living? Since I only worked at night, I didn't have anything to do during the day but play Nintendo. At 22 years of age, I thought my life was pretty awesome, although it lacked the same cachet as being a stockbroker in West Palm Beach.

It didn't really hit home how far the situation had deteriorated until one of my roommates asked me if I was ever going to get a life. She had a point. I'd been having fun but I could tell this was going nowhere fast. She suggested that since I was so full of shit I would be great at sales. Hmm, I thought, she might be onto something. "I work for a company doing inside sales over the phone. I think you'd be great," she encouraged me.

So I went for an interview at the company, a telecommunications giant which is still in business today. Then I went for another interview, and another…you would have thought I was being considered for a position in military intelligence again. After a total of six interviews, I finally got the job. It paid $9,000 a year plus commissions to sell phone book ads.

Wow! For the first time in my life I was earning a salary! Plus a bonus! I worked in an air conditioned office! I got to wear nice suits!

My first day at that job was in November, 1990. And that's where I would spend the next 15 years of my life, clinging with all I had to each rung on the corporate ladder. But I remained true to myself – it wouldn't be long before I got bored with this career, too.

CHAPTER THREE:

EVERY DAY
WAS MONDAY

Joining the corporate world wasn't as bad a decision as joining the army, but for a free spirit such as me, it wasn't the ideal choice, either. Before I left this career, I was promoted to a management position for the first time in my adult life. I'd decided to get out of sales and opted for the higher ranking position of manager (which translated to less money and more work) but after a couple years of this I became extremely tired of it once again.

They say that those who can sell, sell, and those who can't sell, teach. The other managers at the telecommunications company were all former sales reps who couldn't make their quotas. I was one of the few executives at the company who was great at sales but wanted to take a shot at managing people because I was uninterested after achieving top numbers. In the spring of 2000 I'd just finished a six figure year as a sales rep after starting at the very bottom rung of the ladder making phone calls 12 hours a day. Several years later I got promoted and won the employee awards possible along the way. So that was it – there was nowhere else to go. It was either stay on my plateau or move into a different position. I chose the latter.

At the time I made the decision to move into management in was the first week in April and my wife, Angela, was four months pregnant with our first child. It wasn't an easy time; she was suffering complications from the pregnancy and her doctor put her on bed rest. Although there wasn't anything specifically wrong at the time, her obstetrician wanted to keep an eye on her progress.

Angela and I arrived at our first sonogram appointment with high hopes of seeing the little life forming within her for the very first time. We'd get to see our baby moving onscreen, to watch his or her little fingers and toes and maybe even be able to tell if it was a boy or girl!

I held onto my wife's hand as the sonogram technician entered our exam room and hooked up the probe, then smeared a viscous jelly on Angela's tummy. The technician kept one eye on the sonogram monitor as she exclaimed, "There he is!" Sure enough, there he was (we were sure it was a "he"), plain as day, curled up in that strangely baby-like pose that even tiny fetuses naturally take. Now that we could see our baby, it made Angela's pregnancy seem more real. We were both high as a kite. I felt my wife squeeze my hand even tighter. She was so beautiful, lying there on the examination table. I know that millions of babies are conceived every day, but this was the first one I'd had any part in and I was inordinately proud.

I was still getting used to my new job because it was my first week as a manager. I'll never forget that, because things went downhill fast.

The technician's face twisted into a weird expression, her mouth downturned and a furrow of worry etched between her eyebrows. The energy level in the room, so palpably high just seconds ago, evaporated into thin air. "Wait one second, please. I'm going to grab another tech," she explained to us. I rubbed my wife's hand and gave her a nervous smile to reassure her, although inside I was scared to death.

When the second tech appeared and glanced at the screen without a word, Angela and I became even more worried. The second tech came back in the exam room a minute later. Without preamble, she gave it to us straight, "It seems the amniotic sac has ruptured and the amniotic fluid is leaking out."

I didn't grasp the implications of this right away. Angela was only 18 weeks pregnant…she couldn't be ready to give birth, right? "What do we do now?" Angela's worried face was glued to the tech's expression, which remained grim.

"There is no fixing this," she responded. "You must deliver the baby. The baby can't live in your womb without the amniotic sac."

What started out as the greatest couple weeks of my life, learning that Angela was pregnant and getting promoted to a management position, quickly turned into the worst time ever. Time stopped as the sonogram tech informed the doctor, who called ahead to the hospital to admit Angela.

Once she was safely ensconced in a room at the hospital, Angela was hooked up to an IV machine that dripped drugs into her system in an attempt to induce delivery. Our 18-week-old baby was going to enter this world, ready or not.

My cell phone rang before Angela's admittance to the hospital had been processed. It was someone from work, calling to ask me about the graphics needed for an advertisement going into the next issue of the phone book. Then another call came as I followed the gurney wheeling Angela to her room. This time it was an executive from the company calling to complain that a couple of sales reps in my division weren't getting back to their customers in a timely manner.

"Do you know where I'm at?" I practically shouted into the phone. I realized I was scaring Angela so I allowed the techs to continue wheeling her down the hallway while I held back and slipped into a waiting room. The answer? Sure, everyone at work knew where I was but they needed me NOW. I shook my head while doing my best to answer the exec in a somewhat normal tone of voice. All I wanted to do was scream. Did I deserve no respect?

THE JOURNEY TO MAKING EVERY DAY A SATURDAY   53

It was the first week in my new job and I
was already being given a trial by fire, hunted down
at the hospital while my wife and I tried to deal
with the agony of seeing, and then losing, our first
child. It wasn't the fault of the individuals making
the calls; it's just what I'd signed up for when I
sold my soul to the corporation that provided
my paycheck. I was the manager at corporate
headquarters now. Not only did I have to worry
about my own performance at work, I had ten sales
reps beneath me who needed coaching, training,
scheduling and, well, managing.

After what seemed like a hundred years
in the hospital but was really only three days of
nervous tension and pain, Angela delivered a baby
boy so tiny he fit in the palm of my hand. My wife
cradled the baby in her arms, then handed him to
me. The last thing I wanted to do was hold this
baby that I knew was not destined to be in this
world for long but I simply couldn't cause Angela

any more pain than necessary by refusing. I took Matthew into my arms and felt his little heart desperately hammering against my palm. I fell in love instantly.

A priest at the hospital had come by to baptize our tiny little boy. I knew I shouldn't have held him. I was already attached when I handed him back to the doctor. Angela and I whispered a soft goodbye to Matthew while we waited for his little heart to quit beating.

Four hours later, at two a.m., Matthew went home to heaven.

Just a week earlier I'd gotten my first major promotion at work. Now here I was, walking away from the hospital with my wife, a bag of prescription medicine, and an empty baby blanket.

Driving home from the hospital I felt blindsided. What the hell had just happened? I'd been on some crazy roller coaster for the past several days, starting at the top of the ride before plunging down to receive the brain-numbing news of my son's imminent mortality. Now what?

I shook my head. This was crazy. Angela is the one who had to deliver the baby yet I was the one unwilling to accept what had just happened.

There will always be adversity in life. Some adversity is easier to plan for, then there's the kind that comes as a gut punch. When you have to deal with that kind personally, when you are the one taking the big hit, you realize that while your world is falling apart, the rest of the world just keeps on going. That's life. That's how God made it. Sometimes you get a shit sandwich you can't refuse – you just have to take a bite and swallow down that nasty, stinking, putrid meal, like it or not.

At home with my wife after those five days in the hospital, there were five days' worth of bills in the mailbox and five days' worth of messages on our answering machine. The world had, indeed, kept going during our absence. Either we could do our best to catch up to it or we could get run over. I took a few more days off from work, but the following Monday I was back at the office.

Angela and I were luckier than some couples. After a few months, by the grace of God we got pregnant again. This time it was easier, it had to be. We had to trust that our first experience with parenthood was a freak accident. Our first daughter, Madeline, came into this world right on cue. Angela's water broke on Saint Patrick's Day while we were enjoying a meal of corned beef and cabbage. Madeline was born healthy and happy on March 18, 2001, exactly on Angela's due date. I didn't know it then but this gorgeous little girl would be the one who really started Every Day is Saturday. Yet, if Matthew hadn't been born and then died mere hours later, Madeline wouldn't be here now.

It's really difficult, if not impossible, to see the big picture when you're right in the middle of the frame. It wasn't until that one fateful day when Madeline asked me if tomorrow would be Saturday that I could look back and realize that 11 years earlier, everything had happened for a reason. Every Day is Saturday might never have been launched had Matthew been alive. He might never have asked me that same question. This was the way it was all supposed to work out – God's perfect plan.

Not happy with what you've got right now? Just wait; it's bound to change.

Chapter Four:

Location, Location, Location

After the birth of Madeline, I spent a year at corporate headquarters figuring out the whole management gig. It didn't take me long. I became one of the company's top managers by hitting every sales objective given to my division.

I worked hard at being the best, at least for a while. Now that I had a family to support, I figured I couldn't just follow every new whim. My goal was to be the first one in the office in the morning and the last one to leave at night. I arrived at work every morning by four a.m., long before anyone else, and stuck around until my employees had gone home (upper management generally left first so it was easy staying longer than they did). I had to be sure there wasn't even a close second when it came to top performance in the company. It wasn't about a desire to earn more money or gain the recognition of my superiors, I just had to push the envelope because that's who I am – I need to be constantly challenged.

I didn't care what it took, I decided that after the first three months of management experience, my next challenge would be to strive for a promotion to executive manager. I just wanted to see how far I could go. I was already the best manager in the company in terms of performance and the executive team knew it.

Try as I might, the promotion never came. The problem was that the opportunity never arose; the position never became available.

I'd been a part of the management team for two years by this time and I was getting itchy. No one at the company was worrying about granting me the promotion I so clearly desired.

I knew myself well enough by this time to recognize that I needed a change of pace. I started to look for moneymaking opportunities on the side. The entrepreneurial bug was beginning to bite. I surfed the 'net and read through the ads in the back pages of magazines looking for the right opportunity. At one point I was carefully perusing a big print ad showcasing gumball machines when my supervisor walked into my office. I pointed at the glossy, four-color photo of a glass sphere filled with giant balls of colorful gum. "I can put these things anywhere and all I have to do is restock them once in a while to make money," I smugly proclaimed with a thump of my finger to the page. My supervisor shook his head in disgust. "Gumballs? Sam, are you out of your freaking mind? Get back to work!"

One day I was sitting in my buddy Ron's office, shooting the shit. He was a fellow sales manager at corporate headquarters. He mentioned that just the night before he'd been watching a real estate infomercial on late night television. "Do you invest in real estate, Sam?" I shook my head and he continued, "You ever heard of this real estate guru? He's coming to town Wednesday and I got two free tickets to go see him. How'd you like to be my guest?"

Why not?

Two days later when Wednesday rolled around, I found myself excited about the night's seminar. This, I was sure, would be the launch pad to my new career as a real estate investor! Forget those lousy gumballs, this was a real opportunity to make money and set me free from the world of corporate bullshit.

Outside, an insistent mid-April downpour made the roads slick with oil and left splotches on our suit coats as Ron and I headed on foot to the Omni Hotel in downtown Cincinnati, several blocks away from the corporate office. In addition to the time commitment at the end of a typically long work day and the fact that we didn't have a car, slogging through the torrential storm to the hotel presented just one more reason not to go to this real estate guru's seminar. So why was I there? I was *motivated*. When you're as ready to make a change as I was, you'll do whatever it takes to make it happen.

By the time we arrived at the Omni, my buddy and I were soaked. We gave our names at the registration desk and slid into the back of a typical drab hotel conference room that functioned as the chute for a big cattle call. There were at least a couple hundred people there from all walks of life, aged 17 to 70, males as well as females. I sprinted past them all to the front row so there would be nothing in between me and the speaker. I firmly believe this is where you should sit for every event in your life, whether it's a church service or a classroom. It allows you to connect to the action without any distractions.

The guru and his pals were a bunch of slick salesmen dressed in thousand dollar suits. "Jonah", a guy with perfectly coiffed hair and a manicure to boot, took the lead. He reeled us in like fish on the end of his line. He said all the right things, telling us how easy it was to buy one property and then another.

Although the majority of the people in the audience were probably as broke as the day was long, the salesmen on the stage deftly tugged at their heartstrings. It was the first time I'd heard the phrase, "Have you got too much month at the end of the money?" I found myself nodding along at all the right moments. *Yeah, that's me, Jonah! What can I do about it?* Watching his movements and gestures and animated speech, I decided right then and there that I wanted to be just like him. Whatever this guy was selling, I was buying. Literally.

Jonah advertised a three-day real estate boot camp at the end of the month to immerse ourselves in the business of making money by buying and selling property. It cost only $4,995 for three days packed full of all the information we needed to become successful real estate investors. But wait – because we were attending this seminar this night in Cincinnati, these guys were willing to give us a $3,000 tuition allowance just this once! It would only cost the paltry sum of $1,995 as long as we met Jonah's partner, Slick Willie, at the table in the back right away and signed up.

I didn't hesitate. My legs were springs as I bolted from my seat and sprinted to the back of the room. I would be the first one to take advantage of this fantastic offer before it was no longer available. I purchased my spot at the boot camp and returned to my seat with a satisfied smile.

Ron was sitting there waiting for me when I got back to my place in the front row, eagerly scanning my golden ticket. "Look! It says here I can bring a guest! Do you want to come with me?"

He shook his head slowly in disgust. "You've never been to one of these before, have you, pal?"

The boot camp training was a month away but it felt like 10 years as I waited for the first day of the seminar to arrive. Now I had a purpose in life. I was no longer just the manager of my sales division, I was going to become Sam, the wealthy real estate investor. The general gist of the training would be how to buy the right properties, rent them out, deduct expenses out of this stream of income and pocket the rest. It sounded pretty simple. As long as someone could show me a few shortcuts and tricks, I was positive I could make it work. Acreage in the Northeast was scarce and no one was building land so buying existing real estate there had to be a good investment.

The first day of boot camp finally rolled around a month later. The event was scheduled for a three-day weekend so I had to take Friday off work in order to attend. Ron and I drove to a new, generic hotel conference room for the boot camp. I once again pulled him with me to the front row.

I was hooked from the first minute the conference was officially in session. Over the course of the weekend we learned all about making good investments, flipping properties, how to buy mobile homes...my head was swimming. I went home Friday night with two books to read. I am not a reader, but that night I couldn't sleep because I was so excited to delve into these books, especially the one titled *Rich Dad, Poor Dad* by Robert Kiyosaki. I started reading it that very same night and couldn't put it down. I managed to squeeze in a couple hours sleep but went right back to reading the book Saturday morning, gathering bits and pieces of the message that when you think differently, you will act differently. And when you act differently, your life will change. I finished *Rich Dad, Poor Dad* Saturday night, a record-breaking feat for a non-reader like me.

The next boot camp exercise assigned was to go home that night and call all the customer service departments for all the credit cards we owned and ask them to raise our credit limit to $100,000 per card.

What?

"Just do it," Jonah firmly encouraged us. "Ask for more but settle for less. You'll take $25,000."

Back in those days, financial institutions were practically begging customers to take their money. My buddy, however, was unimpressed. "What a great idea," Ron mentioned to me sarcastically. "That way when they try to sell you on the even more expensive program tomorrow, you'll have enough credit to pay for it." I told him to quit being such a downer.

I called all my credit card companies that night. The first one I tried was American Express. I was able to get my credit limit upped to $25,000 on that card. I had the same luck with MasterCard and Visa.

Luckily my wife trusted me so we didn't even need to have a discussion about this new venture. I wasn't trying to hide anything from her; I just knew she would be okay with it as long as I didn't do anything too stupid with these higher limits on my credit cards.

The next day of boot camp when Jonah asked us who had a success story, I was the first one to raise my hand and shout out, "I got $75,000 in credit!" All of a sudden Jonah's eyes narrowed and his lips curved up in a smile. He was nearly licking his lips in anticipation, much like a spider considering the fly neatly trapped in his web.

Ron was right. When they wrapped up the final day of boot camp training, we were each given a diploma and the "opportunity" to purchase admission to a longer seminar and every live event in the future. Another option was signing up for Millionaire University for an additional $2,000.

The salesmen working for the real estate guru left us with a final, encouraging thought. "Everyone here has all the information necessary to buy their first property. I want each of you to go out and start making offers. Only three of you in this room right now will probably do this, but those who do will become wealthy beyond imagination."

I left the boot camp that night with one key motivational phrase on my mind: "When you have the vision to look for opportunities, you will look at everything differently."

When I got home, I reviewed the copious notes I'd taken at the seminar. I called Discover Financial Services and applied for a credit card; not only was I approved but they gave me a $20,000 line of credit in the form of a check with an expiration date 60 days out. That was all I needed to buy my first property.

I decided to go shopping in my old hometown of Bradford, PA because real estate there was much more affordable than in Cincinnati. I had a buddy there whom I called and asked about the possibility of buying some dilapidated property worth $20,000 or less. Sure enough – there just so happened to be a property on the market that fit my requirements exactly. I bought my very first rental, a duplex in Bradford, courtesy of Discover Card.

It wasn't in very good shape, but I expected nothing more for the purchase price. The rental income was $700 per month. So I wrote myself a check for $20,000 funded by the Discover Card incentive and deposited it in my bank account.

That night I dreamt a SWAT team was pounding on my door. I fully expected to be arrested. This was too easy. Surely there was something wrong with this money! But no, I was just being a moron. The sale went through without a hitch.

I knew from my three-day investment boot camp that all I really needed was control of the property. After that, there were plenty of options – I just had to pick one.

I bought the duplex using the $20,000 as a zero percent interest loan from the credit card company. In six months I refinanced that amount and paid off the credit card without paying a dime of interest to Discover Card Services. My mortgage on the property was $180 a month and after expenses were deducted, I was netting $350 each and every month. I'd just given myself a $3,600 raise for doing nothing but signing a piece of paper. As a mid-level manager, I would count myself lucky to receive a five percent raise at work. The average salary of a manager at my company, was $60,000. A five percent raise, or another $3,000 annually, was something most corporate managers would kill for and I'd just assured myself more than that via one easy transaction. This was pretty cool stuff!

I was beginning to understand wealthy tycoons like Donald Trump and Sam Walton, But I identified even more with Ray Kroc, the founder of McDonald's, who always claimed he was actually in the real estate business because his restaurants were all located in high dollar, high traffic locales.

I turned into a fanatic businessman. I received my second promotion at work right after closing on that first duplex and I became the operations sales manager in charge of an entire department, about 50 reps. Things were really humming. In less than 90days, I bought another

18 rental units with no money down, using the investment techniques I'd learned at boot camp, for a total of 20 rentals. The following year that number was up to 28 units. By the year 2005, I owned 40 units, all in Bradford, all purchased with no money down and all due to my showing up that fateful, rainy night for the first real estate seminar. And my interest in that was all due to my typically high level of boredom. I'd wanted a way out of the corporate grind bad enough to take the initiative and do something to change my life.

Shortly after I began flipping properties back in my city of residence, Cincinnati. I sold the condo Angela and I were living in and bought a beat-up ranch-style house built in 1980. I was making pretty good money at that time and I had excellent credit; I could have bought any kind of home for my family but instead I opted to purchase this god-awful property where an elderly lady had passed away.

Although my wife is really good at going along with whatever plan I devise – saintly, almost – this time she wasn't so sure she wanted to back me. "Why on earth are we in this house?" she asked the first time she stepped foot in our fixer-upper special. "You don't know the first thing about being a contractor."

"It was a great deal," I responded sheepishly, shrugging my shoulders and giving her the sad puppy eyes that melt her heart every time. *(What's that, honey? You don't...you've never...my sad puppy eyes don't do it for you? That's okay, this is staying in the book.)*

Angela spent a solid week cleaning that place, from the ceilings on down. It smelled like stale cigarette smoke and the basement was a soggy mess from a recent flooding. We had to replace every single window along with the floors and paint until our hands were numb.

Renovating the place wasn't as easy as I'd first thought, especially while we were living there. The beauty of my plan, however, was that with $18,000 a month in rent plus additional cash flow from multiple streams of income, I could afford to make the much needed improvements. And through my investment business, it was a write-off on my taxes, an added bonus.

One thing I learned from this experience was that cash is king. The goal was to have control of everything but own nothing personally. This was a key piece of information I hadn't learned anywhere else, not in college, not at work, and not from my family.

My friends and family, by the way, were completely against the idea of my new real estate investing business. "You're buying what? You're going to manage all those rental units long distance? Tenants are a terrible burden!" The amount of discouragement that met my new financial goals was extreme. But I didn't listen. I knew my family expected me to be "normal" but that's the last thing I wanted.

In order to be successful, you have to change your mindset and find opportunities just waiting to be capitalized on (thanks again, Robert Kiyosaki) – those opportunities that the average person either can't identify or won't act on. The reason I do everything is to let people know there's another way to live. I break the rules because I can (as long as I do so ethically). When people ask me why I do anything, I always respond with, "Why not?"

That disapproval spilled over into my work life, too. Word quickly spread around the office that I was investing and making myself a nice little income on the side. This rubbed a lot of my coworkers the wrong way. It's not that they couldn't do the same thing; the only difference between me and them was that I was looking for opportunities and making the right decisions. But they didn't have any problem telling me what they really thought, showing me in no uncertain terms the jealousy and judgment they couldn't help but impose on me and my lifestyle.

A big lesson I learned from this experience? If you are seeking approval from others, you will never get it. As the old song goes, you can't please everyone so you've got to please yourself. In the corporate world, you are required to please others: your subordinates and your supervisors. You are squeezed from both the bottom and the top. As an entrepreneur, on the other hand, you only have to worry about your clients, customers and tenants – whoever pays you. Trust me, it's a liberating feeling to be in control and I can't imagine ever giving that control back to someone else, no matter how bad any of my business enterprises gets.

As you are no doubt aware, the real estate market in the U.S. went south in 2008 or so. Of course, it affected me. I had to uproot my family and move them back to Pennsylvania where I could keep an eye on my rental properties. No one wanted to move from their current positions when the market crashed so I couldn't find anyone to manage the properties for me and they became a big albatross around my neck.

I went back to my hometown and collected the rent, shoveled the sidewalks and mowed the lawns. I moved my family into another project home. After several years of incredible highs, we went through some pretty incredible lows.

But was it all worth it? Absolutely. Investing in real estate became my out, it provided the impetus to leave corporate America the first time, and taught me quite a few important life lessons along the way. It wouldn't be the last time I started something new, but it was certainly the beginning of many entrepreneurial ventures.

Chapter Five:

The Impulsive Investor

We all tend to make impulsive decisions when we are faced with undue stress, it's just the way we're made. Our fight or flight response kicks in and we are forced to instantly decide on things that could have a lifelong effect. For me, it wasn't so much the stress of running a $90,000,000 division of the telecommunications company that owned my soul, it was the way my work habits affected my family.

It was a cold, dark November evening in 2004. I had recently received my third promotion in four years, continuing my climb up the corporate ladder, one slippery rung after another. Everything I ever wanted, or thought I ever wanted – stock options, company car, health insurance, expense account, corner office – I had. But there's always a price to getting everything you think you want. In my case it was turning into the person I'd always vowed never to become. When your goal is to reach the top of corporate America, you have to play the game the way it's been written. You either suck up to the execs and become their idea of the picture perfect employee (one with no life outside the office, willing to take on any and every challenge or project) or you won't win the game; that's just the way it's been created.

I knew I wasn't alone feeling that my career was consuming my life. Most of us are dissatisfied with our jobs, to a large extent due to the fact that our talents are unrecognized and underutilized. That was definitely me back in 2004. I knew my talent was to inspire and motivate and empower people. I wanted to blaze my own trail, to be a leader, not a follower. It wasn't in me to be a lemming, to follow my colleagues off the cliff of originality and straight into the abyss of monotony. That was everything I never wanted to become. But that is exactly what was expected of me in order to succeed in a big corporation. If I wanted job security, I needed to tow the line.

I went home that night after being beaten into corporate submission one more time. After making that lonely half hour drive home through the dark, cold November night, I walked into my house immediately bombarded by the acrid smell of burnt chicken. I made my way into the kitchen and lifted the lid on a pan left to warm two hours too many and realized my wife, who is a fabulous cook with a culinary degree, had burned chicken fajitas for dinner. I'm sure they were quite tasty two hours earlier but now all that was left were pieces of charcoal fused to the pan.

Even though Angela had called me at work and asked me what time I wanted dinner, I hadn't told her the truth. I gave her the appeasement answer of, "Half an hour , tops!" knowing full well that this night probably wasn't going to be different from any other; the phone would ring off the hook and emails would shoot into my inbox well after five p.m. Last minute crises were common and as usual, I stuck around to handle them long after everyone else in the office left. The next thing I knew, I was two hours late for dinner.

Angela wasn't mad, necessarily, she was resigned to my late nights. But my oldest daughter, Madeline, was three and a half-years-old at that time and she didn't understand why she never saw her daddy; it wasn't unusual for me to miss her and our three-month-old Laura's bedtime. As I wearily regarded the mess in the pan, Angela came up behind me. "Madeline just went down for the night. Maybe you can still catch her before she goes to sleep."

I dragged my tired ass up the stairs and peeked in Madeline's room, my eyes resting on the fluffy stuffed animals and soft, pink sheets and all the things a little girl needed for comfort. I must have made a noise because she opened her eyes. I perched on the side of her bed as she sat up, rubbing her eyes with chubby fists. "Hey, Daddy." She impatiently pushed a strawberry blonde curl from her cheek and focused her attention exclusively on me.

"Hey, Madeline. How are you doing? How was your day at preschool?" I did my best to make conversation with a three-and-a-half year old who was now awake past her eight p.m. bedtime. That decision to chat with my daughter before gulping down a plate of burnt chicken fajitas, however, would change my life forever.

Madeline cocked her head, ignoring my questions while asking one of her own, "Daddy, is tomorrow Saturday?"

"No, it's not, Honey…but you ask me that all the time. Why do you ask?"

"Because it's the only time you and I get the chance to see each other and spend time together."

You know what? For a guy who had all the answers every day at work, I couldn't seem to find an appropriate response. Madeline's innocent words were a gut punch that came without warning; it took the air right out of me. What was I doing at work every night that was more important than playing with my daughter?

There was only one way I could reply that would allow me to sleep that night, a promise that changed the entire course of my life. "Madeline, tomorrow isn't Saturday, but I promise you that one day, someday soon, every day will be Saturday. That's my promise to you."

I gave my daughter a kiss on the cheek and walked out of that room with my head spinning. I laid down in my bed. I didn't even take off my suit. I just laid there, staring at the ceiling for hours. I couldn't sleep then or the rest of that night, wondering how I could step off the treadmill of my career. How could I ever keep my promise to Madeline? How could I do something that matters with my life and not be like everybody else struggling to make ends meet while working at some mind-numbing job?

That night, tossing and turning in bed, my plan began to take shape.

It was time to reach for my dream of becoming an entrepreneur. It was time to ditch the restraints of the corporate world, to turn in my playing token and declare the game over. That was the good news. The bad news was that I really didn't have a blueprint or any type of playbook to guide the game I was crafting for myself. No one in my immediate family or circle of friends were entrepreneurs. There was no one from whom to get advice. I was on my own from here on out.

I quickly realized that finding someone who knew the ropes would be imperative to my success and that, at least, was a wise decision. When the bridge on the road ahead of you is washed out, you need someone to tell you, "Hey! The bridge is out up ahead." Without that warning system, I would be driving blind and heading straight for a cliff.

And that's why I decided the best course of action was to buy a franchise. Although I'd given some thought as to how I'd leave the job no one else would ever consider leaving, I still didn't have a plan in place three months later. I felt I'd been indoctrinated into the mafia for life, not allowed to ever leave the corporate office because I'd already been gifted with all the benefits and perks I could expect. It was now my turn to spend the rest of my life as an indentured servant paying the company back for all of it.

With my focus on getting to my last day of work, I knew that becoming an entrepreneur

THE JOURNEY TO MAKING EVERY DAY A SATURDAY

would be my ticket to freedom and the only way to keep my promise to Madeline. I was in "buy a business" mode and decided a popular sandwich shop franchise would be the way to go. Yes! That's what I was talking about – my ticket out of the corporate grind once and for all.

I was more than happy to put myself in debt for the next 30 years of my life as I filled out the paperwork with a sense of accomplishment. In mid-January, 2005 I went to the appointment at the bank to close on my very own business, a full time restaurant.

Why did I pick a restaurant business, in which I had no experience? Why did I opt for an operation that opened at 11 in the morning and closed at 10 p.m.? Why did I think I could be successful in a business that required me to be there 80 hours each week – especially when I was still holding down my regular corporate job? Why did I buy a place I simply drove by on my way to work each day without stopping in, afraid of what I'd find? As I've mentioned, I tend to be impulsive and that's what this first stab in entrepreneurialism was – an impulse decision.

It was doomed right from the get-go. I hired a manager to run the place so I could squeak by on spending eight hours a week or less at the restaurant. In hindsight, Jimmie, the manager, shouldn't have been put in charge of a lemonade stand. Even though I was available to run the business on weekends, I stayed as far away from the place as possible in order to avoid disturbing the gigantic ball of doom rolling around in my stomach at the thought of finding out what was really going on there.

That didn't prevent me from having to take care of the business, however. Many times I would be ensconced in a corporate board meeting discussing the balancing of a $90,000,000 budget or how best to incentivize the 70 or so employees under my supervision and the office manager would pull me out of the meeting to give me an urgent message from Jimmie. When I called him back, the "emergency" was something along the lines of "We ran out of ham." I'd give Jimmie my credit card number, tell him to place the order, and then return to my meeting.

All the time I was wondering what I'd gotten myself into. I was already in a job I hated and now I also had the responsibility of a business that was just one more headache that I didn't need. What I needed was an exit plan, pronto. But I couldn't let my business go under because I would lose everything I'd invested into it – all of my savings from my corporate job.

Winter turned into spring and the restaurant continued to go downhill. By May of 2005, things were turning desperate at the corporate office and I was getting antsy for change. Things weren't going to get better with either situation on their own; it was time for me to take action.

That fateful day started out like any other. I was on the phone at my day job, on the receiving end of the "gift of feedback". My boss was telling me everything we (actually I) could do better in the organization. He was blabbering on and on about morale improvement and quality indicators and all those buzzwords on which he placed a great deal of importance, but ultimately meant nothing. It was like listening to the teacher on a Charlie Brown cartoon; all I heard was, "Blah blah blah blah."

I couldn't stand it any longer. I interrupted him mid-sentence. "I quit."

It was almost as if the sound of screeching tires coming to a sudden stop and the smell of burning rubber came through the phone line, as if my boss had been racing along the feedback roadway when he encountered an unexpected speed bump named Sam Crowley. It took him a moment to recover, to turn his thought processes 180 degrees around. "What are you talking about, you quit?"

"I quit. That's it. I'm done."

"What do you mean you're done? You can't quit. You run the largest division in our organization. Why would you quit? What's wrong? Where is this coming from?"

I tried to explain to him that I just couldn't do this anymore, how my daughter wanted every day to be Saturday, how my heart simply wasn't in this job anymore and how my future definitely did not include receiving the gift of feedback. I tried to tell him I was no longer interested in being the lowest common denominator and certainly had exhausted the thought of throwing a warm blanket around people who can't handle the day-to-day responsibilities of their jobs. At work I had 80 direct reports; at home I had two of them:

Madeline and Laura (with another one on the way) and I'd decided they were my top priority.

It sounded good, but on the inside I just wanted to throw up. I couldn't believe that after working for the same company for 15 years and climbing that steep corporate ladder, I'd thrown it all away with two words. But it was done. I couldn't un-ring that bell. I just had to rip off the Band Aid® and be done with it.

I was now officially out of a job. It was both the greatest and the scariest feelings in the world, both of them jumbled up together and causing havoc in my already troubled stomach. I had two kids and a third on the way in five months. What the hell was I going to do?

For the next couple of days I couldn't eat or even function normally; nights with no more than a couple hours sleep were common. I was asked to keep my defection from the corporate mafia on the QT until the execs figured out how to handle the situation.

In the meantime, my self-talk kept piping up at inopportune times to remind me of the folly of this snap decision. Who would quit a job that involved being in charge of millions in revenue, earned a handsome salary in addition to a bundle of perks, and didn't require any travel? Who was that dumb? Me, that's who.

Eventually word of my defection swung its way around the office grapevine. One of the execs scheduled a mandatory meeting for the entire division a few days later, my last scheduled day of work. Mandatory meetings were not usual and this one was described as an "employee announcement" that would affect everyone in the division.

The night before the meeting the impact of what I'd done really hit me. *Holy shit! I won't have a job after tomorrow! I've got two kids and my wife is due with number three in five months! What the hell am I doing?* It was impossible to sleep with all those feelings of guilt and uncertainty eating at my gut.

Angela and I made the decision a long time ago to never put the kids in day care; our goal was for Angela to raise our kids, not some stranger in a daycare facility. So she was on board with whatever decisions I made as long as the goal was to 1) spend more time with my family; and 2) gain financial freedom. That was the litmus test and my decision to quit my job passed that test. Some of my plans didn't always work out this way, but as long as I was doing things for the right reasons, Angela never once complained.

The guilt and uncertainty I felt over my decision tasted bitter in my mouth, however, after I considered what I'd given the company those past 15 years. I was always the first person there each morning and the last to leave at night. I'd worked weekends and gone above and beyond the call of duty. Yes, I'd been rewarded with three promotions in five short years, representing my ridiculously fast climb up the corporate ladder. But maybe that was the problem. Maybe I'd just burned my candle out too quickly. Then again, it could be that deep down inside, my inevitable boredom was making another infamous appearance.

The attendance at the next day's meeting was as expected; the room was filled with dozens of familiar faces. Some of them glanced at their watches every few seconds, others checked messages on their cell phones, while others yawned and headed for the coffee carafe in the back of the room. It looked like a normal meeting in the midst of a busy day until the announcement of my resignation as division manager. Eighty heads in the room turned as one and gaped at me, most of them in shock. I was definitely in the spotlight at that moment and not for a good reason. After all, I was Mr. Corporate, the last person expected to leave a good paying job with all the benefits. It was time to get this all over with once and for all; the bandage needed to be ripped off as quickly as possible.

"Let's bring Sam up to say a few words."

Right on cue, I gave my first motivational speech. I didn't blink, I just went right into a spiel I hadn't rehearsed. The words came from my heart and I think my audience knew that when I faced them and began. "It's been great 15 years working with all of you and I've had many wonderful opportunities. But I want something more out of life. My daughter wants me to make every day Saturday for her because that's when we get to spend time together. That's my goal: to make every day Saturday for my family. I don't know what I'm going to do exactly, but I'll definitely continue to focus on real estate."

I stopped short, swallowing hard. All of a sudden it really hit me that I would not see these people again. We'd been through a lot together. I was respected as "everyman", the kid without a college degree who'd worked his way up the ladder ethically and with honor. I was one of their own. My voice cracked and my mouth was full of cotton as I struggled to finish my impromptu speech.

I needn't have worried about my reception. I received a standing ovation. Everyone who worked for me came up afterward and gave me high fives, slapped me on the back, and wished me lotsa luck.

The warm and fuzzies didn't last long, however. On their way out the door of the meeting room, someone said, "I'm just so sad Sam is leaving!" I overheard the CEO of our partner company reply, "It's no loss. I never really thought his heart was in it anyway." In just seconds, the guy had managed to show his other face and it just confirmed my decision to leave. I didn't say anything at the time but it registered in the back of my mind that I never wanted to work for someone like that again. I could never respect a man who compromised his morals so blatantly and I certainly didn't want to turn into him, either. This guy was everything that was wrong with corporate America. Someone who only respected others based on what they could do for him.

I returned to my office after the big meeting. I sat down in my cushy leather chair for the last time and boxed up my things. It took forever because people kept coming in and telling me goodbye with tears in their eyes. It made me realize what a big impact I'd had on others' lives. The corporate execs, however, didn't get all mushy about my departure; the only thing they were concerned about was grooming my replacement. Other managers who had left under different circumstances were granted a going away party and given a gift of appreciation. Me? I got nothing. The execs were pissed off that I was leaving on my own terms and thus deemed I didn't deserve a lovely parting gift. This was just one more indication that I'd made the right, albeit impulsive, decision.

I held my head high when I left that office building and I even whistled a happy little tune. For the first time in 15 years, I was in control. The only things that would happen in my life were those things I decided. I was now in the front car of a roller coaster headed for the peak of the hill. Most people never reach that apex. But I knew I had to get there; I couldn't live with regret.

Luckily, the thought of regret was more of a motivating factor than fear over the course of the next year or so, although at times those two were running neck and neck.

Friday I said goodbye to my corporate job. Monday I reported to a sandwich shop in Columbus, Ohio for training. I wasn't allowed to run my own restaurant because it was failing miserably so the corporate muckety mucks of the franchise decided

I needed a bit (a lot) of help in the form of training at a successful store.

So Monday morning I showed up at the Columbus restaurant at (almost) nine a.m. wearing a black visor, a polo shirt with the franchise logo and a pair of khaki pants. I had to drive 90 minutes one way just to learn how to run my own business alongside a bunch of college kids, learning how to make subs.

Traffic was tough and by the time I arrived in Columbus it was a few minutes after nine. I was greeted by a short guy with a complexion the color of strong tea named Samir, whose first words to me were, "You're late."

Who did this guy think he was? I'd just quit a C-level executive job, a better one than he'd probably ever dreamt of having.

That didn't seem to faze him. "I'm your trainer and I own this store. You need to be here at nine instead of nine-thirty." Samir reminded me of the Soup Nazi from *Seinfeld*. "You got to take a test or you can't work here," he continued, undaunted by my scowl. "You need to know how to make subs, how many ounces of ingredients go into each sandwich. It is my job to teach you. Start by taking the test and let's see how you do."

I skimmed over the questions. The first one asked how many ounces of marinara sauce go on a Chicken Parmigiana Sub. I didn't even know we sold a Chicken Parmigiana Sub. Needless to say, I didn't do so good, scoring a 30 percent out of sheer luck. After 15 years of corporate management experience, I wasn't even qualified to work at this sandwich shop, a point which Samir brought to my attention in no uncertain terms. "You cannot make sandwiches here with a score like that."

I squared off against all five feet five inches of my sub shop nemesis. "Look," I told him. "I just quit my job. I don't have another source of income. I have to do this training to run my own store.

Call whoever you have to call but I'm working here today."

The seconds ticked by as Samir assessed me with a critical eye. I squinted my eyes at him and he furrowed his brows in response. The theme music from *The Good, The Bad and the Ugly* cued up inside my head. After a few more tense seconds, Samir picked up the phone and spoke with the regional franchise manager. Samir nodded his head and I sucked in a deep breath, realizing I'd been holding it. *Yes!* The regional manager okayed the continuance of my training.

My first day on the job at the Columbus store I learned how to wrap subs. There's a particular way to fold the paper around each sandwich so customers could easily unwrap it – and see the prominently displayed franchise logo. Who knew? From there I graduated to more complex duties. I learned that two people actually make the subs and each sandwich motors through the toaster for 57 seconds. When it comes out the other end, I had to ask the customer, "Do you want lettuce on that? Then I would wrap the sandwich in printed paper with the logo facing outward so it was the last thing I saw. I was feeling more confident as each hour wore on. How hard could this be?

The restaurant opened promptly at 11 a.m. There were two teenagers with piercings stationed at the "make table" sending subs on their journey through the toaster to me at the other end. As I reached for the first one, I smiled smugly. "Do you want lettuce on that?" I asked the customer. Piece of cake!

By 11:30, there was a line of customers snaking around the corner of the building. Subs were now flying through the toaster. Fifty seven seconds felt like 57 minutes as a roomful of hungry people stared at me, waiting for their lunch. I gave up on asking about lettuce and just jammed each sandwich into its wrapping this way and that, desperate to get them off my workstation and into to-go bags. Have you ever seen that episode of *I Love Lucy* where she and Ethel go to work in the candy factory to earn some extra cash? That was me on the sub line. The only thing worse would have been rabbits flying at me.

Samir was onto my sloppy ways, however. He would rip those nonstandard sandwiches out of my hands and take the time to add lettuce, then rewrap them nicely, with the corporate logo facing outward.

By two in the afternoon, I was drenched in sweat, my visor sideways, gangsta style, shirt untucked and I felt like a wrung out dish rag. How did I end up here, getting screamed at by a short Indian guy while wrapping subs made by 19-year-old dropouts? I felt more stressed by Samir then I ever had in the corporate world. *What am I going to do for next two weeks? Two days ago I was making decisions for a billion dollar company.*

Now I was being told to sweep the dining room. Should I laugh, cry, leave, quit?

Unfortunately, I still had to make the 90-minute drive home to Cincinnati and then get up and do this all over again for the next 20 days.

By the second week I got promoted to the make table and it was finally my turn to send subs through to the new guy on the other end of the toaster.

By the third week, I got the hang of making subs from start to finish. Samir finally warmed up to me. I started to get my self esteem back. Although I was only taxed with small responsibilities and stupid ones at that, I felt proud that I'd made it this far in the world of making sub sandwiches. After three weeks of training, I took the test again and scored 100 percent. I was now ready to run my own restaurant!

Back at home in my own store, I tried to insert my thumb into an ever-widening hole in the dam. The first thing I did was fire every employee except Jimmie, the manager, to whom I felt I owed more to after all those months of ignoring him and the store. Within thirty days, using my training and the management skills I'd honed in the corporate world I got the rudder turned back around in the right direction.

Unfortunately, it was too little too late. No matter how hard I tried, there was no way I could hit the numbers necessary to pay the bills. I gave it a valiant effort, though, wearing an Elvis costume and even an inflatable suit to attract customers. There I was, Mr. Corporate, standing on the sidewalk in a ridiculous getup with a fan blowing up my backside to inflate the suit, trying to dodge cars that got suspiciously close to the sidewalk when they passed my post. Even Angela got into the game; at seven months pregnant she would stand out front of the restaurant holding a sign that urged traffic to come in from the heat and enjoy a freshly made sub sandwich.

At least I could say I tried. There's only one shot at life., one shot to squeeze that last little bit of toothpaste out of the tube. Are you up to it? Are you going to go for it?

Let me tell you something: if you make that decision to stay where you are and never go forward and never dare to be great, you've got no reason to bitch and moan. You got to own it, man. You have to absolutely own it or stop complaining, one or the other.

I haven't eaten chicken fajitas since 2005. Truthfully, I can't stand the smell of them after that night when dinner was burnt and I realized I'd let my family down by making them less than my first priority. And sub sandwiches? They're not my favorite, either. Dining restrictions aside, I gave it my all. I made impulsive decisions, but I owned them and I owned up to the fact that they weren't necessarily the best decisions. No regrets, right?

CHAPTER SIX:

DOWN BUT NOT OUT IN CINCINNATI

Fortunately, I'm able to take a bit of criticism and I can even readily accept being humbled, like I was in Samir's shop when I realized I wasn't even good enough to assemble a sub sandwich. I'd been down before and chances are I would be again. But little did I know that the biggest dip in my career was yet to come.

After returning to my restaurant in Cincinnati and setting myself to the task at hand, the sales numbers turned themselves around dramatically. I went from almost no sales to a much healthier amount. Mine was one of the worst stores in Cincinnati, always at the bottom in terms of sales numbers. In just 60 days, I'd managed to increase sales a good 40 percent. But that was just like chipping a sliver off the iceberg in front of the Titanic. I needed to do twice that amount just to make a profit. It was still bad but not as bad as before.

It was enough to grab the attention of the bigwigs at the regional franchise headquarters, who lauded my efforts to bring my store up from the bottom rank and called me on a daily basis to tell me what an amazing turnaround I'd brought to my store. In fact, they wanted to give me more stores. While my ego was tickled pink, the writing was on the wall. Unfortunately, I still owed a huge bank loan from the purchase of the restaurant. I was working seven days a week but was forced to pay my mortgage and grocery bills with credit cards that were quickly maxed out. My wife was due to deliver our third child in mere weeks and my COBRA benefits, at a whopping $1,200 per month, were just too expensive to afford. So, we had no health insurance and my business wasn't making enough to cover my family's cost of living. Something had to change, and fast.

For a while I thought about toughing it out. *Is it that I just can't do the job? Or do I need to stop the bleeding, cut my losses and swallow my pride?*

Although I hated to do it, I finally gave Angela the low down. "I'm worried...the store is doing horrible and we're losing money." She had no idea how bad the situation was because I'd sheltered her. I was the man of the family, the person responsible for everyone's welfare. I needed to be big and strong and bring home the bacon. At this point, however, I was lucky to bring home a can of Vienna sausages.

My ego was at war with my common sense but in the end, the loss-cutting, pride-swallowing course of action won out. And I knew what that meant. I took a deep breath. I had to call my old boss, a senior executive and ask for my job back at the telecommunications company I'd given 15 years of my life to, and then snubbed. He might say no. He might talk it over with the other execs and give me the bad news accompanied by a big old ration of shit on a shingle. There was certainly no way I could get my old job back. After I left, a small faction of underachievers amidst some really great former co-workers were only too happy to stab me in the back on my way out the door.

It was the last week of August, 2005, just three months since I'd give my motivational farewell speech to the masses. I put on my big boy pants and called my old boss, Dan. "Hey…are you looking for any sales reps? I know you have a big campaign starting soon and I'd like to help you out." I thought that maybe if I couched my request in this way, it wouldn't be so obvious that I'd just experienced massive failure.

"Sam? Why would you, who used to run the division, want to come back as a sales rep?" Dan's tone was incredulous but tinged with just a hint of smugness.

I hemmed and hawed and finally blurted out the truth. "Please don't tell anyone the real story but my restaurant failed. My wife is due to deliver our third baby any day now and my COBRA benefits are just about up. I really need this job, now."

Dan affected his "corporate tone" and harrumphed as he replied, "We're going to have to have a meeting about this. You had rental properties and you were doing entrepreneurial stuff on the side last time you worked here. Everyone remembers that, Sam. Some of the sales reps are bound to be less than happy to see you return."

Not long after our conversation Dan called me back with the news I was dreading to hear but needed to hear just the same. "Senior level management had a meeting about you, Sam.

Your replacement, Rob, who is now running the division, called in all his sales reps and asked them their thoughts. They were kind of supportive... As long as you aren't made a senior account rep, everyone seems to be fine with you returning to the company."

Yes! I would have a stable income again, a bit of breathing room with the bills, and I could get my health insurance back.

My relief was short-lived. I thought I'd be welcomed back to my old division with open arms but that wasn't even close to what happened.

After leaving with a cushy salary of $100,000 I was now returning as a sales rep with a base salary of about a third of that much. Rather than the plush corner office I'd once occupied, I was now relegated to a tiny cubicle just like all the other worker drones.

But before I was allowed to make the walk of shame and sit my butt down in a cubicle, I had to fulfill one requirement. "You can't just return without an explanation, Sam," Dan explained to me over the phone the night before. "You need to tell the whole division why you've come back. You owe them all an explanation."

The last time I'd been on Interstate 71 was driving home after my farewell speech. Now here I was on the congested freeway once again, returning to the office, only this time rehearsing my "I'm back!" speech, which made me far more nervous than the "Sayonara" one.

As I walked through the door of the familiar office suite, I was welcomed back, but not everyone offered tidings of good cheer. Every manager I'd hired and later denied a Christmas bonus for failure to make quota, every sales rep whom I'd put on suspension due to some infraction of the rules – those few jealous sorts I'd pissed off were there waiting for me, my new peers and bosses, with a smirk of malicious glee on their faces. I was walking the Green Mile with a big target on my back. Along the way I passed my old office, where Rob now enjoyed the view I used to relish. I was just Sam the sales rep, no longer Sam the division manager. My pride was a big lump nearly impossible to swallow. But I had to…I needed this job more than the company needed me back.

I gave the politically correct speech I was required to give then I got down to work.

This time my motivation was different. I wasn't at the office to make friends or influence people. I was there to work, and that's what I did. I went in early and got right down to business selling advertising and closing accounts. It wasn't long before I became the number one sales rep in the division.

And right on the heels of this success was a demonstration of insane jealousy from the rank and file.

No longer was I just Sam the sales rep, now I was Sam the zoo animal, on display in my cubicle. Everyone was looking at me – and talking about me. I heard the gossip. And I quickly learned that if someone is gossiping *to* you, they are gossiping *about* you. It's going to happen. The only way to combat it is to put your head down and do the job you're there to do.

I worked during the day and at night I researched bankruptcy online. I needed to know what would happen to me if I filed Chapter 7 or Chapter 13. I needed to know my options. I still had a huge amount of debt from the restaurant and no way to pay it off. Now that I had my job back, I had to consider how in the world I was going to handle the hundreds of thousands of dollars of debt I'd amassed.

Right after returning to the company, I called a bankruptcy attorney. Of course, I had to make the phone call from my cubicle, well within earshot of all my co-workers, giving them one more way to rub my failure in my face. I set up a lunch meeting.

The first time I met with the attorney, I didn't know quite what to expect. Although I'd done my research, I didn't really know how the whole ball got rolling. "I guess I'm not making any money," I explained to the lawyer sitting across the desk. "I have no idea how this whole process works. Talk to me like I'm a five year old. At this point I think people who file bankruptcy are real losers."

We talked at length. I'd brought along a shoe box full of bills from credit card companies. The attorney took one look inside and frowned. If he'd been a medical doctor, his diagnosis would have been terminal. "The laws are changing on October 18th. It won't be as easy to declare bankruptcy then, so I suggest we get started now. Chapter 13 is the best route; that way you can keep your rental properties and pay a percentage of your debt back to the creditors."

Holy shit! I'm really going bankrupt! Now *I* was one of those losers.

The first step for my self esteem was to get comfortable with the thought of bankruptcy. I did some more research online and found a lengthy list of millionaires who'd been in the same situation as me, at least financially. Rather than thinking of myself as a loser, I thought about it being the first step toward becoming a multi-millionaire. Yeah, that's right. I was just like Larry King, Michael Jackson, Donald Trump, Mike Tyson, Marvin Gaye and Mark Twain, all of whom filed bankruptcy at some point in their careers.

My daughter, Paige, was born October 5, 2005. I filed bankruptcy just six days later. I was in tears as I left the attorney's office. I couldn't believe that just by signing a statement, I'd turned over nearly $400,000 in debt. I felt as if there were a big scarlet "A" for Asshole sewn onto the front of my shirt.

When I got home that night from work, I sat down heavily on the couch, bringing all my burdens with me into the house.

"Daddy!" Madeline shouted as she ran at me full bore, arms stretched wide. Six-day-old Paige was in my wife's arms and Laura was crawling on the floor nearby, perfectly content to examine a piece of popcorn. Three kids and a house and we were now bankrupt. I looked around at all of them, feeling the tears welling behind my eyes. I never cry. My kids have never seen me cry. I had to keep it together.

"Are you all right?" My wife asked me later, after the kids were in bed.

"I don't know how this works, Angela," I admitted. "Am I allowed to go to the ATM and get cash? There's someone controlling how much I spend from now on."

Angela gently rocked our youngest daughter in a cradle next to our bed and looked at me with pure love shining from her eyes. "You've got us," she gently reminded me.

That's why I love my wife so much. She was right. I had a beautiful, wonderful woman at my side and three healthy kids. It was time to turn things around, to take this negative experience and turn it into something positive.

In bed that night I prayed. "God, give me one more shot. Take it all away...I'll never mess it up again. I'll never buy things I can't afford to impress other people. Give me one more chance and I'll do it better next time."

I returned to two parallel lives the next day with a renewed sense of purpose. I had a job to focus on and a bankruptcy to get behind me. I broke the record making quotas while being a leader in the sales department. It didn't matter that everyone hated me; my day job was what would get me out of this mess.

At night I gathered all the information the trustee requested to prepare for the first creditor's meeting scheduled in a few short days.

One of those creditors was the guy who sold me the sub sandwich shop and he was pissed. He'd already taken a loss on the sale, now he was only going to get a fraction of the remaining debt back. Then again, he wasn't honest about the store's numbers either, and that's why I could never have made the business profitable.

The Cincinnati Bankruptcy Trustee Office is an eight by ten room that looks more like a prison cell than a conference room. How apropos! Present at the creditor's meeting with me were my attorney, the trustee, the seller of the restaurant and his attorney.

Someone pressed the record button on a tape recorder and the meeting began with me swearing to tell the truth, the whole truth, and nothing but the truth or face jail time.

Was I really a criminal? All I had wanted to do was be an entrepreneur. Why was I here?

The trustee was a lady wearing tortoiseshell, cat eye-framed glasses and a ready smirk, who also did a lot of loud talking and gesturing. From my point of view, her job was to make this meeting as miserable as possible while doing everything in her power to keep my bankruptcy from being confirmed. In all actuality she was just doing the job she was appointed to do, working for the other side and trying to get as much money for my creditors as possible. That meant trying to stop the proceedings from going forward.

What irony! Up to this point, I hadn't wanted to go this route; I'd wanted to avoid the big "B" word at all costs. But now that I was here, I was all in. I was ready to give up the fight to pay my bills and declare bankruptcy but the people sitting across the table didn't want to let that happen!

The meeting continued with a financial autopsy. Cat Eyes went through my bank statements, my credit card bills, my receipts – nothing was off limits. "You owe $30,000 on an American Express?" She shook her head as if to say, "What a moron!" I was in front of a firing squad and Cat Eyes was directing the bullets.

Where's this? Where's that? The intention of the meeting was to intimidate me and in that regard it was quite successful. In most bankruptcy cases, no one shows up to the creditor's meeting. It was just my luck that I had a creditor with a huge ax to grind and a trustee who resembled Rizzo in *Grease*.

I didn't think I could sit through another one of these meetings but another was scheduled anyway, for December. This time Cat Eyes wanted to see appraisals of all my rental properties.

My Christmas gift was in the form of the restaurant seller not showing up at the meeting. Still, I was forced to sit in that dark, dingy basement of the federal building in Cincinnati with the trustee and the seller's attorney. According to my lawyer, he was a high-priced litigator who was once a trustee himself so he knew all the ins and outs of bankruptcy.

This time I was grilled for another hour and half. The meeting lasted so long we all took a break. During a Chapter 7 filing, it's all pretty straightforward; it takes about 10 minutes to do a cut and run. My meeting, however, went on for more than 90 minutes, far longer than usual.

"This guy is going to try and hit you up for $150,000, which you said you had in cash," my attorney informed me during the break.

My stomach was queasy when we returned to the meeting. Luckily that $150,000 was part of my 401(k), so the trustee couldn't touch it.

The creditor's attorney did his best to catch me in a lie. He went through each question (and there were lots), purposely wording them in a way that would make me stumble. I was onto him, however, and I wasn't a liar or a cheat. As I answered each question, my confidence grew. All I was doing was using the law to protect me, which was well within my rights. I hadn't gotten into debt with the thought of never repaying it. I was a good guy.

By the end of January, I still had not received confirmation of my Chapter 13 bankruptcy. There was no final meeting yet scheduled because the trustee kept putting it off. I prayed to God again, asking Him for His help in getting through this. *Please, Lord, let this end!*

The last meeting on my bankruptcy filing was finally scheduled. It was a warm day for February; the sun was shining and I felt confident that my plan for paying back my creditors would get confirmed.

When I got to the courthouse, my attorney wasn't there yet. *Oh, great...I've been waiting for this day to arrive for months and now I'm on my own? They'll probably have to reschedule...*I glanced at my watch every few seconds and tapped my foot on the institutional beige linoleum. The bailiff called us into the courtroom. Where was my lawyer?

At the last moment he came flying through the door, coattails flapping, like Kramer entering Seinfeld's apartment. *Thank you, Lord.*

My attorney and I entered the courtroom, along with the trustee, and the proceedings got underway. My creditor and his attorney weren't present so there were no objections to my plan.

Before I left, Cat Eyes had a bit of sage advice for me. "Next time you want to do anything entrepreneurial, I suggest you don't do it at all or you get some really good advice because you obviously don't know the first thing about how to run a business."

"Yes, ma'am," I replied solemnly.

I was merely placating her. As I left the courthouse, I handed a check to my attorney for his services, then sauntered down the street, whistling a merry little tune. I was on my way to a café down the street to meet a friend of a friend whom I wanted to hire to design my Every Day Is Saturday website.

Try as she might, the trustee couldn't keep me down long enough to call me out. No one can take me down because I don't care what they think. I've had my share of tough times and they've left me battered and bruised, but it wasn't as if I could never recover. Resiliency is the name of the game if you want to become an entrepreneur. Learn that now and you'll avoid a lot of stress later.

CHAPTER SEVEN:

YOU CAN GO HOME AGAIN... BUT IT'S NEVER THE SAME

Some people are fond of saying that you can never go home again. That's simply not true. You can go home any time you want – you just can't expect things to be the same as when you left. For me, going home means not just returning to Bradford, PA, but anywhere in the general vicinity. Small towns tend to be like that – they take up more space than just the city limits. But there, just like everywhere, time passes and people change. I did...I know I went from being a poor kid from a little burg to a corporate "bigwig" to an entrepreneur and motivational speaker with a worldwide audience.

But going home doesn't just apply to returning to your hometown. The work environment is a "home", too. After declaring bankruptcy and losing my franchise operation, I went home to a cubicle at the office where I'd worked for 15 years. It didn't matter that I'd only been gone three months; people change even in that short amount of time, which for me felt more like years rather than months.

Going home to the corporate office was a real wakeup call. I always thought the place couldn't run without me but it did. I didn't think I could be replaced but I was. I thought I'd be welcomed back like an old friend but I wasn't.

Yep, a lot can change in 90 days. It wasn't like being gone a decade and returning for a high school reunion. This time going home meant I was starting all over again as Sam Crowley, the brand new sales rep. It would have been better if I'd never worked in the place before. I thought 15 years of experience would be a help but it actually hurt. This time I had a bullseye on my back. If anyone could do anything to upset my apple cart, they did.

I didn't realize just how difficult it was going to be to come back to work until I was there and ensconced in my little cubicle. I was in the same building, using the same elevator to reach my division's floor, parking in the same parking lot only this time I showed up with new baggage and a new title. The rules of engagement changed. I was no longer Sam, the lovable guy who'd worked his way up the corporate ladder through hard work. Now I was Sam, the sales rep, the arrogant, cocky guy who'd gotten his comeuppance after all. And everyone at the office was more than happy to witness it.

Yes, I was back in the same place but the environment was different. From that first day back, I battled the fact that I was going through bankruptcy, my next child was on the way within a matter of a few short days, and no one there cared. I was a mess inside but somehow I managed to gather myself together each day and do my work. It was kill or be killed. I was bigger than the gossip. It was time for me to show up and lead by example.

It was a requirement of the job that every new hire be trained on required computer work, such as uploading daily sales reports. The irony was that I was trained by the manager I'd hired. General orientation was much the same story; I was schooled in the corporate culture by a supervisor I'd hired. Although I'd once run the whole show, I was now just a grain of sand in the big old beach of a company.

After a half day of training, I was allowed to return to the floor housing my cubicle by the prison guards. Heads looked up from their computer screens and conversations stopped as I passed by. I could tell by the energy in that space that everyone was thinking, "I can't believe this guy came back after that speech about Saturday…" It was another humbling experience for me. I had to learn how to be just another sales rep in a cubicle.

After my first day back at work, I came home and told Angela how strange the whole experience felt. She wasn't surprised; she had known it was going to be awkward thanks to office politics. But I just didn't have a choice, I had to focus on making money and getting structure back into our lives.

I refused to allow that bad energy at work to get to me. So I wasn't welcomed back, that was okay. So everywhere I went I was subjected to quizzical looks. So what? I wasn't back in the cradle with a warm plush blanket.

The adversity I was feeling was actually beneficial. No one gave me the time of day and that allowed me to focus solely on "crushing it" in regards to goals and quotas and numbers. I didn't need to prove anything to anyone other than myself, and I sure as hell didn't need corporate politics or help from any corner to further my career. I wasn't there for the long haul anyway. This was just a temporary setback.

Every month I worked after returning to the company, I absolutely crushed the competition in terms of meeting my goals. The funny thing was that I never got the Employee of the Month award. During an entire sales campaign, I was named the number one rep for most of the year and received recognition for that, but I never did get that Employee of the Month award. The decision was made by the management team and the protocol was for the honored employee to receive a plaque and a check for $100. It was all symbolic and didn't mean a thing to me, but not so for those people who took great satisfaction in preventing me from receiving the award. Obviously I had made this pseudo part time job look way too easy.

I was shattering the earnings ceiling and nobody was happy. I had hired every one of those 'judges' and denied them an annual bonus at the same time asking them to come in and work on Saturdays when necessary and they'd never forgotten that, either.

Finally, after beating every rep in the division for seven months straight, I was given the dubious honor of being named Employee of the Month. As soon as I got the plaque, I tossed it in the trash can in my cubicle. I realized my performance wasn't based on possible recognition from corporate muckety mucks. Winning awards and representing my division as a leader by example became a sour note. There was no joy in it.

That was also the reason why I didn't attend when the division manager invited me to a get-together at his house. It was an invitation coveted by everyone in the sales department and I declined it in favor of spending time with my family. I was around the people at my place of work not by choice and I sure didn't need to hang out with them on my personal time. Even then I began to realize that if I wanted to reach new heights, I couldn't spend time with people who would drag me down. It's not that I'm an Elitist, but this fundamental principle is what got me to the other side of success. If you surround yourself with people whose expectations are so high that you must raise your own expectations to meet them, you will go so much farther in life. And the reverse is true, too. Spend time with jealous, tired, bitter people and you'll turn into one of them.

My story could have been anyone's; those of you who are right now working your way up the corporate ladder need to decide that you will take the first step toward becoming an entrepreneur and follow through with it. Find your passion and your purpose. You could jump off the ladder and fall flat on your face. That's what I did, so I went back to the comfort zone of my old workplace. That's always a possibility, but it's nothing to fear.

My problem at work wasn't due to anything I'd done or said. In fact, I'd stayed in touch with many people at the company over the three months I was gone. We'd exchanged emails, many of them inspirational, encouraging me to keep pursuing my dream. The problem when I came back was that I wasn't supposed to come back; I was supposed to be gone for good. I used to be a mentor and a great influence on others in my division, now they were competing against me for the same bonuses, awards and recognition. They didn't have any idea how difficult it was; how everything I did and said was being scrutinized and dissected by everyone around me. Those inspirational emails I'd been receiving just weeks before now turned to negativity and gossip: "Shit…he's back."

Many of my coworkers knew I was working on developing Every Day Is Saturday from my cubicle. That wasn't received well. In fact, I had a picture in my mind of all of them huddling in the break room around steaming cups of coffee, wondering how in the world I could dare to be motivated and inspired from the confines of a cubicle.

It's important to realize that if you ever want to go back to your comfort zone – those things or people you know best, whether it's a town, a romance, a friendship, a marriage, an organization or a job – it will no longer be that comfy place or a fond memory. Once you've decided to change, the dynamics in a relationship or a situation change. Unless someone really loves you for altruistic purposes, without wanting anything from you but willing to help you for the sake of your own good, they won't understand why you left in the first place. They have not changed while you have. They haven't achieved what they wanted to during your absence. But that's their problem.

They can either accept the new you, or they can do everything possible to sabotage your efforts at a new beginning. Unfortunately, you are likely to find more of the latter so be prepared.

You can go home again. But your home will never be the same because you aren't the same. But that's not a bad thing.

CHAPTER EIGHT:

SATURDAY BEGINS TO TAKE SHAPE

I rang in the new year of 2006 from the confines of my cubicle. Another year had passed and there I was, still waiting to turn my passion into my livelihood. I would sit there in my chair, facing the institutional blue carpet-covered wall, and think about my website named after my daughter Madeline's poignant request.

I did a Google search and found that every EveryDayIsSaturday.com was already taken. Did that stop me? Did that derail my progress? Nope. I decided that I would get that domain name, no matter what the cost.

By searching the website Whois.com, I found the owner of the domain, whose name was John, living in Oregon. He had bought the name back in 2000 and it was now six-years-old without a live web page; it was just a parked domain. That was a good sign.

I decided to contact John but not via email; I wanted him to hear the passion in my voice when I pleaded for the domain name I'd dreamt about for over a year. I called the phone number I'd also found via Who Is. Many times the information registered with a domain name is either old or wrong and I fully expected to hear a recording telling me the number had been disconnected. I didn't hear that recording but another one asking me to leave a message.

I thought quickly. I had thirty seconds to convince John that I needed his domain name more than he did. As soon as the beep signaled the beginning of my message, I went into action. "Hi,

John. My name is Sam Crowley. I live in Cincinnati. I was looking for the domain name, every day is Saturday dot com and I see that you already own it. You see, John, my daughter, Madeline, asked me two years ago if tomorrow would be Saturday because I was working all the time and Saturday was the only chance she got to spend time with me. I promised her that one day I would make every day a Saturday. I have to keep that promise to my daughter. Not only do I want every day to be Saturday, I want to motivate and inspire others worldwide to do the same thing. That's my dream, John. Please call me." Just for good measure, I gave him my phone number three times.

I barely got the entire message out before I heard the second beep indicating my time was up. Whew! Had I said the right things? Was my story going to resonate with John and convince him I needed his domain?

Fortunately, I didn't have to wonder for long. The next day my cell phone rang. I glanced at the display on the screen, not recognizing the number. I cautiously flipped the phone open. "Hello?"

"Sam? Hi, this is John. I own every day is Saturday dot com."

Oh my God! John! "Did you get my message? The whole story? The dream?"

"Let me tell you something, kid." John's voice was mellow; he sounded like somebody's grandfather and I immediately began to relax. "You've got something special there. I bought that domain name several years ago when I retired and I thought I would share what I was doing each day with my friends. But you've got something amazing. I wish I had made the same decision you did, had the same ambition when I was younger. I tell you something, I want you to keep your promise to your daughter, Sam. I'm going to give you the domain name."

I didn't say anything for several seconds as I waited for his words to sink in. Then I let out a whoop of pure joy. "I will keep my promise to my daughter, John, and to you, that I will make every day a Saturday. I appreciate that offer, I really do. Thank you."

I gave John my email address so he could transfer the domain name to me. I sent John $100 via PayPal to thank him for his generosity.

Was it simply luck that allowed me to get that domain name? I don't think so. I'd taken a shot, a stab in the dark, by calling up a complete stranger and pleading my case. But that just cemented the benefits of sharing my message. I learned that when you have the opportunity to share your story with someone else, you never know how it's going to resonate. John was a father, and he understood my message and my promise to a little girl who could just as easily have been his daughter.

Now I was in business. I paid a local firm way too much money to build my website. You might wonder how I was able to pay thousands of dollars for a website when I was in Chapter 13 bankruptcy and couldn't even get enough credit to buy a soda. All that effort I was putting in at work wasn't just to break records; it was the method of financing my dream. I was squirreling away as much as possible each payday so I could fulfill my mission of monetizing Every Day Is Saturday. I gave the website designer a nice down payment and paid the rest via installment payments over a few months.

That first website had a blog, naturally, so I started writing posts right away. I added my phone number and email address and asked visitors to contact me for speaking engagements. I also asked them to let me know how my blog affected them.

I was doing everything possible to engage visitors and make them want to return to my website.

After a few months of regular blogging, I received an email message from "Fred Jackson". The gist of his message was, "Hey, great to see you're making every day a Saturday but are you sure you're being completely honest? I know you work in a cubicle and make phone calls for a living."

Hmm, apparently "Fred" was someone with a vendetta who wished to make fun of me via a public forum. I searched for the IP address from which the message was sent and found that it was associated with my workplace. Surprise, surprise.

When I got the second email from Fred Jackson I decided to reply to him (or her). My response to Fred let him know that I wasn't sure exactly who he was but I did know he worked at the same company I did. Unless he wanted me to uncover his real identity take the evidence to

Human Resources, I suggested he stop sending messages. I ended it with a trite little sentence about him living his life so I could live mine and hoping that his got better.

I thought it was best to alert my division manager that I was being harassed online and I did just that. I thought he needed to know that I was continuing to research Fred Jackson's corporate identity. The manager's response? "You do have a business you're trying to run on the side, Sam. Are you using a company computer for this investigation?"

That's all the guy was worried about – my use of company resources. Heck, Every Day Is Saturday wasn't even a business back then; it wasn't bringing in any money. It was little more than a blog. I was providing motivation via the Internet and I never said anything bad about my workplace. But the manager didn't want to hear any of that. He saw what I was doing as a huge threat to his job.

Fred emailed me back and denied that he worked at the same company I did. I knew better. One of my coworkers had recently done the same thing – started his own website. He got a message from Fred Jackson, too. Obviously, going after a dream had put us both in this guy's crosshairs. It was no wonder. I'd never gotten a harassing message when I'd been the division manager, someone seen as a "lifer" in corporate America. It was only because I was now an average Joe, putting myself and my dream out there for anyone to see, that I'd attracted someone as jealous and bitter as old Fred.

The anti-Sam behavior was no longer limited to office protocol, it was now coming in the form of emails to my personal address. I couldn't dwell on the situation and allow this harmful energy to negatively affect me and prevent me from achieving my goals. I know that when it comes to bad experiences, you have to deal with them via a three-step process: accept it, then harvest the best and forgive the rest. Otherwise it will distract you and keep you from moving forward toward your real purpose.

This was a new outlook for me. Before declaring bankruptcy, I didn't have a forgiving bone in my body. But now that I'd gone through that whole humbling experience, I could better understand others in a similar boat. I was able to forgive not just nice people, but my enemies, too.

At this point I was one year removed from the end of my bankruptcy repayment plan, and one year in with the same company I'd left in a spurt of rebellion. I had an outstanding month that summer when I reached my quota for sales volume for the entire year in just thirty days. I was driven and focused, tuning out all the stuff going on around me and just worrying about me and my family. I was in the eye of the hurricane, making my own magic and making good things happen.

I've often been asked how I could have returned to that cubicle day after day to take orders from people I'd once hired all while suffering through bankruptcy. In my position, I only needed to focus on what I needed to do. Everything else took care of itself – the jealousy, anger, backstabbing and all that negativity was someone else's problem. I lived minute by minute, not looking back and not worrying too much about what the next day would bring.

I had a bit of money and that was a huge relief. I treated Angela to dinner out that summer of 2006. We hired a babysitter and went to a nice restaurant. We sat at an intimate little table and looked across it at each other. What a tough road it had been to get here. Of course, I paid cash for that dinner because I still couldn't' have a credit card due to the terms of Chapter 13. Still, we were doing better than ever before, comparatively, because I was focusing on what was most important while forgetting all the bullshit. I had only my family to look after – no other people, no budgets, no crazy deadlines. Every Day Is Saturday was finally growing. Just a month later, I would get my first speaking gig. Life wasn't necessarily easy, but it was good.

One way that things were better than ever was due to my detachment from failure. Failure doesn't define who you are; it's a verb, not a noun. As long as I woke up each morning focused on becoming someone unbelievably great, I knew it would lead to something great. But I had to believe it would happen and I had to realize it would take time. Success is like priming a pump; the water might not bubble forth in abundance right away but it's crawling its way up to the spigot and when it finally gets there, it will overflow.

By the time I'd achieved all those pinnacles after returning to work as a sales rep, I was bored. I talked to my former boss about everything that had happened in the past year and told him I would not hesitate to quit again. He was flabbergasted and I had a hard time believing those words were actually coming out of my mouth...again. But things were happening. I had my mojo back. I was blogging and podcasting and speaking at local engagements. While everyone in the cubicles next to me were focused strictly on sales, I was learning the ins and outs of online marketing, search engine optimization and marketing, and how to manage a website. I needed more stimulus at work if I was going to last much longer. I was operating on a different plane and I knew I could bring much more value to the company beyond my current role as a sales rep. So my former boss (now my boss' boss' boss and vice president of the division) told me he'd meet with the other execs and see what he could do.

My boss came through for me. The company actually created a brand new position just for me: Senior Account Website Manager. They were smart enough to realize that e-commerce was the wave of the future so they put together this hybrid job that allowed me to continue caring for a handful of select clients while managing search engine marketing products for the company. They gave me a base salary of $100,000, a big jump from the $39,000 I'd earned as sales rep and even more than my boss and most of the management team earned. Although I asked them to keep my new salary on the QT, word got out within a week.

The eyes were burning in my back again as I walked past. *There goes Crowley, up to his usual tricks*, were the whispers accompanying those stares.

I ignored the additional pessimism coming from coworkers; for me life was good. I gave the company their time and spent the rest of it on Every Day Is Saturday. I woke up most mornings at four a.m. to blog, write articles and eBooks and podcasts for my business. All that hard work paid off. I was dominating the first 10 pages of a Google search for "Cincinnati speaker".

By the end of that year, things started to go sideways at work. I was getting bad vibes from just about everyone. The sales reps I'd worked with earlier in the year were insanely jealous since I hadn't had to pay my dues to take such a big step up the corporate ladder. And I was still making way more money than they were in sales commissions. Management had numerous meetings about me, wondering how I could continue to hit such big numbers with only a handful of accounts left to manage.

It got even worse when the senior vice president decided it was a good idea to send me along on sales calls with the reps so I could sell my search engine product directly to business accounts. This went over like a lead balloon. No one wanted me to ride along with them.

One day I came into the office early and found the executive management team in the midst of a meeting...about me. "Look at Crowley," they were saying. "He's making more money than we are and he's only here three hours a day while we work 12-hour days and weekends!" I stood outside the partially open door, listening and chuckling over their dilemma. They were so focused on me, they didn't worry about what they could do to change themselves. I had put myself in a position once again for people to talk about me because I was achieving things they felt they couldn't.

After the holidays, the division manager called me into his office. I knew this couldn't be good; he wasn't the type to call someone in to give them a pat on the back. He wasted little time getting to the point. "You're putting stuff on the Internet about our company. Did you really call Jeff a moron?"

Well, yeah, I had called that manager a moron but I didn't call him by name. What was the problem? Wasn't the bigger issue that the management team was wasting their time talking smack about me?

That wasn't the division manager's cause for concern, of course. He accused me of trying to turn the tables on him, then reminded me that the entire sales force and management team hated my guts. I was fueling the fire by putting out podcasts and blogging about the insanity going on in the office. In an effort to keep the peace, I reluctantly agreed to stop.

Things still didn't get any better as spring rolled around. I scheduled a meeting with the executive vice president of the company, the second in command and someone I trusted. She was a very smart lady in her late forties who was a corporate go-getter from right out of college. I asked Kathy if she would run interference for me. "Can you just help me succeed in my new job here, Kathy?" I asked. "I've been nothing but a target because of jealousy."

Kathy agreed to help me in any way she could but the writing was already on the wall. Thirty days later she called me into her office at headquarters for a three p.m. meeting on a Friday. Anyone knows that a meeting with a high level manager at the end of the day right before the weekend was not good. Positive communications were scheduled for the beginning of the day so it would motivate an employee to do better. Negative conversations always occurred at the end of the day so the disgruntled employee could go straight home and use the time to get over it.

I strolled into Kathy's office and greeted her as if nothing was wrong. "Hey, how's it going?" In my eyes, this meeting with the executive vice president of the company was like a U.S. senator meeting with the president of our country – not quite on equal levels but understanding each other's position. Everyone in the office had felt threatened when I met with Kathy last time, thinking they would need to take direction from me, the blogger. I had no doubt this meeting had something to do with that.

Kathy got right down to business. "You're doing a good job, Sam, but unfortunately we need to terminate your position."

Her words stunned me. I knew I was doing a good job and moving the company forward, into the future. I managed to find my voice and asked her what had happened.

"You've got too much baggage, Sam. It's becoming a huge distraction to others in the office.

Plus, your sales figures for those thirty accounts you kept are way too low."

Rather than focus on all the sales records I'd broken in the past 23 months, I appealed to Kathy's sense of reason. "Forgive me for disagreeing, but if we don't focus on search engine marketing now, in the next few years we will lose all the business we've built up. We can't rely on phone book advertising sales alone when everything is going online."

Kathy offered me a position as a training manager with a base salary of $60,000 and bonus opportunities that would reach $100,000. It was almost laughable. Then again, I knew she was just following orders to stop the bleeding somewhere in the organization; I was the human Band-Aid®. "Take some time; don't answer right away," she exhorted.

Of course the late Friday meeting gave me enough time to go home and be angry all weekend long.

The following Monday, almost two years to the day since the first time I quit the company, I walked back into the office for the final time. I told my division manager that I quit – this time for good. I assured him, however, that I wouldn't run the company into the ground. What had happened to me was the same thing happening at organizations around the country, even around the world. Depending on which survey you cite, anywhere from half to 81 percent of workers today feel that their talents are underutilized. People get pigeonholed because companies need a warm body in a particular position, whether or not their talents and desires mesh with those duties. The corporation needed me as a trainer, but that would be wasting my talents for internet marketing. If anything, I'd learned more about building an online presence during my few short months as Senior Account Website Manager; my skills were growing and yet the executive decision was to take me out of the arena just when I'd gained the upper hand in the fight.

Where did that leave me? For the second time in as many years, I called my wife to tell her I'd quit my job. It wasn't a surprise to Angela; I'd left that morning telling her that I might stay if they offered me a better position than trainer.

Angela's response was just what I needed to hear. "Great! You are quitting to do what you love to do: personal development. And you've got your website!"

Although her words were meant to cheer me up, I couldn't help but be a bit pessimistic as I drove home. *Here we go again. No income. Nothing to fall back on. No going back this time.* I didn't just burn a bridge, I blew it to smithereens.

The good news was that my lack of steady employment allowed me to focus on Every Day Is Saturday full time, with the same passion I should have shown two years prior. Now I was laser focused. I had to make this work, for my family's sake. I felt like a lion on the savannah with a herd of caribou in sight: I was frothing at the mouth anxious to go after that for which I hungered. Sure, I could go broke again, but I was so dialed in to what I needed to do to achieve my goals that there was no place to go but up.

We all have the desire to return to the warmth and comfort of a security blanket, whatever that may be (a job, relationship, a place). I don't think that's necessarily a bad thing. In my case, no one was happy about my decision to return to my place of employment and they made that more than apparent. In order to deal with all the resultant crap, I had to force myself to operate on a different level. I wasn't even sure I could do it until

I threw myself into work with a kill-or-be-killed desperation. When you have to succeed, when there is truly no other option, you learn how to tune out everything else and focus on the greatness inside. Looking back, I become angry that I didn't realize this 15 years sooner and use that energy to achieve something great for myself much earlier. I could have saved myself so much stress!

Whoever you are right now, you have greatness inside of you. It's truly amazing the positive ways you can react to a dire situation. You probably don't really know just how much greatness is inside until you are presented with an opportunity to show it.

If you don't succeed at the goals you set for yourself, does that make you a failure? Absolutely not! You must earn the right to be called a failure. If you don't take any risks, you can't fail. And if you don't fail, you aren't trying hard enough. If you never experience what it's like to go after a big, crazy dream, you will never be a failure – and that's really sad.

Chapter Nine:

Going Home Again, Part Deux

Are you a planner? Do you feel as if every part of your life needs to be set out in advance and that you must account for every penny of your money, every minute of your time? Then you, my friend, will not make a good entrepreneur. Going into business for yourself requires you to roll with the punches. In fact, you never know what's going to happen next (just ask Angela, wife of a serial entrepreneur). That's the beauty – and the beast – involved in entrepreneurship. You'll see what I mean when I tell you about my rental property odyssey.

Just a few weeks into my second attempt at entrepreneurialism, I received a phone call from the guy managing my rental properties, Tom. He informed me that he really didn't want to do this particular job for me anymore. I was in Cincinnati, my rentals were back in my hometown of Bradford, PA – some 400 miles away. Not only had I relied on my manager to take care of tenant calls, I also used him to help me with my real estate investments by recommending new purchases.

"What are you going to do if he quits?" Angela, always the voice of reason, asked me.

Tom had never mentioned quitting! I'd always told him he better not get hit by a bus because I didn't know what I'd do without him. At this point, it seemed he was lying in the middle of the road just waiting for a bus to come along. Apparently Tom now wanted to do his own thing and start fresh somewhere else. I tried not to sound shocked when Tom gave me the news because I

didn't want him to know how much control he had
over me. Instead, I asked him for some time to
transition to a new manager.

I cut the cord with Tom a little over a month
later, although I had no idea what I was going
to do.

I'd left Bradford in 1998 and never looked
back. I'd never imagined a circumstance where I'd
need to return…until now. It's not that I didn't like
the place, but it was small in every sense of the
word. It wasn't a place with a bustling economy
or lots of job opportunities. The reason I'd bought
real estate there was because property was cheap
compared to other locales. I never imagined that
Tom would leave before the rentals sold or I had a
Plan B in place. But that's exactly what happened.

Angela and I discussed the situation further
at dinner that night. We bandied about a few ideas,
finding another property manager being one of
them, but it all came back to only one viable course

of action: move back to Bradford, PA. I didn't know anyone else to take over as property manager since all my old friends were off on their own ventures, so Angela and I made a list of the pros and cons of moving to Pennsylvania. The pro list wasn't as short as I thought it would be. Hmm…maybe it wouldn't be so bad after all.

Yep, here I was, going home again. And that meant we needed to take the kids out of school and find a tenant for our home in Cincinnati because our mortgage was underwater and there was no way we could sell it.

When we got home from dinner, we didn't tell the kids right away. There were still a lot of things to do, with number one finding a place to live. After filing Chapter 13 bankruptcy just two years earlier, I had no credit. Angela, on the other hand, hadn't been part of the bankruptcy proceedings and had maintained good credit. This was the period right before the big real estate bust and at that time, banks were offering "no doc" loans to anyone with a credit score of 720 or higher. Angela began scouring the Internet for real estate deals while I picked up the phone and started calling my Bradford network.

My first trip back to Bradford, outside of class reunions, was in June, to scout a house. This time was different. I couldn't quite make it all the way into town without gathering myself together. I stopped about 10 miles out because the wave of emotions rolling over me threatened to send my car off the road. The scenery, the scents, the sights, the sounds – they all took me back 20 years. I'd left as a teenager with the idea that I would never be back yet here I was, idling along the edge, almost ready to plunge right back in.

I stayed with a friend during my house hunt. Every day I looked at several properties but nothing seemed to fit our budget or our needs. Tom's last day had been the end of May and in addition to finding a house, I had to find someone in the interim who could take care of maintenance calls, collect rents and deposit the money into the bank. My friends made a recommendation for a temporary property manager and I blindly trusted them because I had no other choice.

I returned to Bradford in July and lo and behold, much like Goldilocks, found a property that was just right. I'd actually spent a lot of time in this house since an old buddy's family had owned it while I was in school. As a kid, I'd spent a lot of time there playing with my friend, Fletch. It was full of memories, but a bit lacking in the niceties. In fact, it needed a ton of work. It was a 3,000 square foot home with an interior reminiscent of the one featured in *The Brady Bunch* but, unlike that house, this one hadn't had any work done in ages.

Never one to back down from a challenge, I put in an offer on the house and it was accepted.

The bank wouldn't close on the property until October but I negotiated to take occupancy early and pay the owners rent for the months of August and September.

In the meantime, I listed our Cincinnati home with a local rental company and asked them to advertise it heavily. There wasn't much else I could do other than trust they would find a tenant – it was wither that or pay two mortgages.

Without having the house leased, Angela and I packed up the kids and all our things in mid-August and left our dream home for Bradford.

As I watched the moving truck pull out from the curb, I took one last look around the house Angela and I had always thought we would die in. All the furnishings were gone, and so were the memories my kids had left behind. They wouldn't go to high school here and they wouldn't see their friends from church again.. Each scratch in the kitchen countertops brought back a memory;

each smudge on the wall marked a moment of my daughters' lives. *Goodbye, house. I can't believe I'm leaving you behind.*

I shooed the family into our minivan while I got into the driver's seat to start the trip back to Bradford. It took seven hours that felt like seven years and the loss of my soul. Although Angela was completely on board with the decision to move, because we really had no other choice, that didn't fill up the empty space I felt inside.

I pulled up to the curb outside our new home, the one I'd practically grown up in. While the movers unloaded all of our stuff, I met with the guy I'd hired temporarily to maintain the rentals. He handed me the keys to all the units. "Here you go!" were his cheerful last words with nary a word of advice.

After sending my tenants a letter that made the turnover official and provided my phone number in case of emergency, I sighed deeply. I was now

Sam, the property manager. It was up to me to fix problems, collect rent and handle disputes.

My trial by fire began almost immediately with a call for a leaky faucet and a toilet that refused to flush. All my plans for Every Day Is Saturday got swept to the side as I put on my cape and rushed around town with a plunger in one hand and a wrench in the other. Managing my rentals became my full time job.

When it came to repairs and maintenance, I pretty much sucked. I tried my best to find someone reliable to take over those tasks for me but ended up going through maintenance personnel like water. I even tried the Robin Hood approach, offering them a higher wage than they could expect anywhere else and giving them extreme flexibility in the hours of the job, but to no avail. If they didn't steal from me, they didn't show up or couldn't do the job. I couldn't find an honest worker to save my life.

I remember this period vividly because it really opened my eyes to a prevalent problem. Although I was practically begging people to take advantage of the opportunity to work full time for an above average wage, there were so many who wasted that opportunity. With unemployment numbers at astronomical heights in recent years I have to wonder how much of that is just plain laziness.

I was in desperate need and much like that corporation had done a year earlier, I grabbed a warm body to fill a vacant slot.

It was Spring of 2008 and I'd been managing my own rentals for the last six months while renovating my Brady Bunch home. Not only had my wife signed the original mortgage to buy the house, she got a second to cover the costs of remodeling. Our living situation had gone from enjoying a beautiful dream home in Cincinnati to making do in this fixer upper special without a working kitchen due to renovations. Luckily, we found a tenant for our Cincinnati home a week after moving; a temporary corporate relocation who needed a place to rent for nine months. At least that took some of the financial pressure off. But while we worked hard in PA scraping wallpaper with a putty knife and painting walls until our wrists hurt, there was some stranger enjoying our gorgeous home in Cincinnati. What was wrong with this picture?

I had more than enough on my plate already so when a tenant of mine expressed an interest in taking over the maintenance of my rental properties, I jumped at the opportunity. The guy needed money and I needed help. I brought Scott on board with a smile and a handshake, relieved to give over the one responsibility I really dreaded.

After a couple months of this arrangement, things started to smell as rotten as a fish on hot summer beach. My new property manager collected rent over the course of a few days each month, a bit here and a bit there, and then deposited the money into the bank. After adding up the bank deposits, I realized some of it was missing. Then there was the call from the local contractor's supply house where I kept a charge account to buy supplies for the rentals. It was their accounting department, asking me to make a payment on a $4,000 bill! *What?* Typically, there was no need to spend more than a $1,000 a month on supplies. The store shut off my account.

I called Scott and asked him what was going on. "I don't know what they're talking about, Sam," was his lame reply.

"All right, then, let's go down there together and get this straightened out," I urged. Scott reluctantly agreed.

At the store, I asked to see all the receipts for the last month. I went through them one by one and it didn't take long to figure out what had happened. The first one was for rental of a backhoe and a delivery of several hundred yards of gravel; that totaled about $1,200. What the heck?

"Did you rent a backhoe, Scott?"

"Yeah, I told you about that. Remember? I told you I wanted to put gravel in the front of my unit and make a driveway."

How did I not know about this? It's because Scott lived there and he'd decided to spruce up his place real nice. Me, being the trusting soul I am, never even drove by to see what Scott had done.

The next receipt was for copper pipe in the amount of $1,200. Apparently that purchase went straight from Scott's truck to the scrap yard. Not only that, Scott had cut out all the old copper piping in the rental units and scrapped it, too, then replaced it with PVC.

I wasn't one to beat around the bush. I demanded that Scott pay me back the $6,000 I could prove he took unlawfully. I threatened to press charges if he didn't comply. Although Scott returned as much of the money as he could, it wasn't nearly enough.

The lesson here was mine to learn. I simply didn't manage this guy closely enough. Scott had said he wanted to buy the unit he was living in from me and use his grandfather as cosigner on a note. He also said he knew someone at the local bank who provided a commitment letter to guarantee Scott could obtain financing for a mortgage. I received that letter of commitment shortly before I found out Scott was stealing from me and that should have been the first red flag – it was written as if by a first grader. The bank later confirmed this, telling me that letter didn't belong to them and there was no one there whose signature matched the one on the letter. That meant there was no commitment from Scott to buy my property and no commitment from the bank to finance the purchase.

It just so happened that while I was at the bank confirming Scott's deceit, the man himself walked up to a teller window. Upon seeing me, Scott turned tail and ran. I ran right after him, anger making me faster than usual, until I caught up. "Do you realize what you've done, Scott? You forged someone's name to get a loan! Not only have you stolen from me, you've committed a felony!"

That was it, the last straw. I pressed charges and Scott was convicted. He was sentenced to two to four years in a Pennsylvania prison.

Of course, this little episode happened in the midst of everything else going on in my life – from moving back home to Bradford, to renting my dream house to some stranger, to renovating my "new" old home. All this while still trying to find the time to work on Every Day Is Saturday; it felt impossible. I was like a fish out of water in Bradford. I liked the place, but it didn't feel right and it just wasn't Cincinnati, the place my entire family thought of as home.

The saga of my property manager woes didn't end here, however. Just a month or so later I was approached by another guy who heard I was looking for help with my rentals. This guy had some experience, having managed properties in Rochester and a few other places. He came at me from a Christian angle, telling me how he was born again after being saved by Jesus, whom he had taken as his Savior. It sounded good to me, so I gave the keys and the responsibilities over to my new manager with a not-so-subtle warning, "The last guy who had this job stole from me and now he's in prison. If you think about stealing from me, I guarantee the same will happen to you." His reply? "No sir. I believe in God. I go to church. Call my pastor if you need a reference."

Unfortunately this guy ended up being just as bad as his predecessors. But I was desperate to get my family back to Cincinnati and willing to do whatever it took to make it happen. Even if he royally screwed up, I felt I could occasionally come back for a few days at a time, and set things straight again.

After things settled down in my hometown, it was time to move back to the big city, where Every Day Is Saturday could really take off. That was my family's real home, the only place my kids had ever known. Less than a year after moving back to Bradford, I loaded up the family and we went back to Cincinnati. As soon as the temporary tenant moved out, we moved right back into our dream home.

Just as I'd been able to go back home again to my workplace, I was able to come back home to the place I'd been born and raised. In the process, I learned that I can do anything I would ever need to do. Although I've never been handy and didn't know the first thing about being a landlord, I accomplished everything I set out to do in Pennsylvania. I took that dark, dank old house with thirty-year-old carpet and turned it into a real showcase, like something that belonged on the glossy pages of a magazine. Even though it wasn't a permanent home for my family, the time spent there renovating it provided me with a real sense of accomplishment.

And even better than that, for the first time in my life I had learned how to face my fears head on and deal with them. I could have let those rental properties go and stayed in Cincinnati. But instead I uprooted my family and got down to business doing what needed to be done. It felt good and it felt right. This was the turning point, I just knew it. Everything from here on out would be a piece of cake, right? Well…almost.

CHAPTER TEN:

DO YOU WANT IT
BAD ENOUGH?

When you become an entrepreneur, the good news is that you are your own boss. The bad news is that you are your own boss.

Let me explain by way of the growth of Every Day Is Saturday.

After moving back to Cincinnati, I'd quit my steady job for the second time in as many years, in order to pursue my dream of speaking from stage and motivating people via the Every Day Is Saturday message. I didn't have any money coming in to speak of, other than my rentals, and I needed to generate a steady income or go broke. I'd managed to build up a bit of savings and keep my 401(k) plan, but I still had horrible credit due

to the bankruptcy. I didn't have any way of getting
a loan, accessing a second mortgage or any other
types of funds. Although I was confident in my
ability to build a business, I was much more afraid
this time around because my safety net was gone;
there was no way I could ever go back to that work
environment ever again. I was truly out on my own
this time, adrift on a river without a paddle, after
setting the bridge on fire behind me.

Even while in Bradford, I continued to
work on my website and online presence as time
permitted so that was still in place while I settled
back in to life in Cincinnati. I didn't have any
speaking engagements yet, so I had to come up
with a product to sell online. While I focused on
tenant issues from seven in the morning until five
at night, I reserved the nights for Every Day Is
Saturday. During the day I often met new tenants
and took a look at my properties for the first time,
noting which lawns would need to be mowed in

the summer and which sidewalks would need to be shoveled come winter.

I held my first Every Day Is Saturday phone-in class in October, which I named the Blueprint Class and advertised as being a six-week course via conference call. I sent a mailing to my small database telling them my first class was open now and the first two sessions were free. *Get in on the ground floor! Make tomorrow and every day thereafter a Saturday!*

I made sure my home office space was all set up with everything I needed. I sketched out a brief outline of what I would cover in that first call on a cold Tuesday evening in October. I logged in online well before eight p.m. and dialed into the conference line I'd reserved, then waited impatiently for participants to call in.

By fifteen after eight I realized no one was going to show. "Angela," I called out the door to my wife. "Go upstairs and jump on this call, all right?"

"What? You want me to go upstairs, pick up the telephone and listen to you talk?"

That's exactly what I wanted her to do. I wasn't going to waste this time. I pressed the record button and went right into my spiel, with only my wife listening. "Hi everyone! This is Sam Crowley. Over the next six weeks, we're going to learn…"

Things didn't get much better for a while. Over the entire length of the course, I had, at most, six people join me live on the calls. Could I have canceled the calls? Sure. But what kind of message would that send to others – and, more importantly, to myself? I decided to do it anyway. Besides, since I recorded the whole thing, I knew I could package it as a product down the road and sell that. It was important that I didn't cancel but kept on going forward.

After that first tele-course, I branched out into other sources of media. I shot videos and started podcasting as a way to reach as many people as possible. I wove these tasks in between maintenance calls for my rentals and desperate efforts to replace my property manager via classified ad. I'd hire a person and two weeks later he would quit. In between maintenance calls and interviews with potential managers, I would pull over to the side of the road and speak into a small recorder I kept in the car. This form of messaging came easily to me and I found myself podcasting morning, noon and night. I tried to stay focused on Every Day Is Saturday all the while keeping one thumb in the dam of rental property maintenance overflow.

Even with all the hassles over management and maintenance issues, I still loved real estate. I thought briefly about getting my realtor's license. That first summer back in Cincinnati I enrolled in a three-week real estate course. It seemed like a good idea at the time. Sure, selling real estate is purely a commission-based income but that didn't scare me. What did scare me was the thought of continuing to pay a property manager while I had no income other than rent.

I went to class faithfully for one week. Then I got the phone call that changed my life forever.

It was a Friday at the beginning of June, the end of the first week of the real estate course. I felt like I was back in college, learning from nine to five, listening to lectures about laws and rules and other dry, boring topics. I came home from class that night with my brain wrapped around abatements, clear titles and mortgage insurance. The first thing I did was head to the phone in my home office and click on the flashing button that signaled I had a voice mail message. "Hi! My name is Heather. My company is looking for a speaker. I know this is short notice and I'm sure you are really busy..." Little did Heather know that I'd just spent the day in real estate class! "Our event is scheduled for July eighth at the Hilton Hawaiian Village in Waikiki. Please call me back and let me know if you are available."

I couldn't believe it. There was someone willing to hire me as a speaker? I was so excited I could barely talk. I forced myself to calm down, then gave myself a pep talk before calling Heather back. *You gotta be on your game, Crowley!* I coached myself.

Heather thanked me for calling her back so quickly. "We have one speaker already, an author who wrote a chapter in *The Secret*. We're interested in you as the speaker for the remaining day of the conference."

The burning question in my mind was how she had found me but I couldn't ask. Instead, I said, "Sure." I would have signed up for this gig even without a fee, but that wouldn't seem very professional. So I asked Heather about her budget for speakers.

"It's about $25,000 for a keynote speech. You'll have to speak in a four-hour workshop. This amount is negotiable, of course."

I tried to come off as if I'd done this type of negotiating and this type of keynote speech lots of times. I assured Heather that her budget was in my ballpark. She informed me the company would pay all my expenses except for airfare. "So, you're available, Sam?"

I fought back the urge to shout "Yes!" at the top of my lungs. I took a deep breath and casually answered, "I don't have my calendar in front of me right now, but I believe so."

Heather told me she would talk to the owners of the company and let me know if she would contract me for the job within a couple days.

That weekend passed excruciatingly slow while I waited for her phone call. I couldn't believe someone was willing to pay me $25,000 for a keynote – and put me up at a hotel in Hawaii!

Angela, ever the practical one in the family, asked me what I was going to talk about for four hours. "I don't know, but who cares!"

When I hadn't heard back from Heather in nearly a week, I finally decided it would be okay to call her. I used my cell phone during a break from real estate class to leave her a message. "Just wanted to say my schedule is getting booked up quickly, Heather. Have you talked to the owners yet?"

She called me back within minutes. "Sorry for the delay in getting back to you, Sam. You're good to go! I'm sending a check for $12,500 overnight to you today and we'll pay the remainder after you've fulfilled the terms of the contract."

I was nearly floating home after hanging up the phone. Just months earlier, in the cold of winter in Pennsylvania, I was shoveling sidewalks so my tenants could get out of their driveways. I would anxiously watch the weather report each night on all the local channels to see how much snow was forecast the next day. Mornings would find me pouring salt on sidewalks to melt the ice and fighting frostbite on my nose and hands. I dealt with evictions, chasing down rent, and people who mysteriously moved out overnight. But I had stayed in the game! Now here I was facing my first big break.

I ended up dropping out of that real estate course for which I'd paid some $1,500. Of course, I never did get my realtor's license but the market crashed just a few short months later, so it was probably a good thing. Besides, I had more important things to do now, like prepare for my first keynote speech. I took this duty seriously, even renting a conference room at a local hotel so I could work on my presentation in peace and quiet.

THE JOURNEY TO MAKING EVERY DAY A SATURDAY

I experienced another fortunate occurrence right about this time. I still owned that house back in Pennsylvania (actually Angela did, but who's keeping track?) and it was vacant. I met a wonderful family in Bradford, a young couple with a little boy who had fallen on hard times and needed a place to live. Although the house was for sale, I took it off the market and rented it to this family. I was honored to be able to help them this way and it was definitely a God thing. God had put me in the position of having gone through a lot of stressful circumstances; now He was giving me the opportunity to bless someone else going through hard times. I understood their plight. I wanted that little boy to grow up in a nice house. Both Angela and I knew it was the right decision to help this young family. And I could now see why we had to go through that experience of losing a property manager, moving back to Bradford and being saddled with the burden of fixing up that old house. That one decision to go back home ended up helping so many: my family, the neighborhood and now this new family.

The conference dates quickly approached. I apprehensively boarded a plane bound for Hawaii and tried not to look like a newbie at this whole flying thing. I'd once gone to Ireland back in 1995 and I had flown some with my corporate job as well but not enough to be considered a frequent flyer by any means. I hadn't been able to sleep the night before and I found it hard to settle in for the long flight.

When the plane finally touched down in Hawaii and I disembarked, I was shocked to find a driver from a limo company holding a sign with my name on it. I tried my best to act as if I expected no less than this, all the while thinking to myself, "I did it!"

At the end of the event, I knew that I was doing the right thing. I knew that I was fulfilling my destiny. Hundreds of people told me I had changed their lives forever after listening to me speak. It was the most amazing experience of my life.

Even on my way back home, on the airplane that departed Hawaii bound for Cincinnati, there were people on the same flight who recognized me. They came up to me and said hello, asked how I was doing. I felt privileged to shake their hands and tell them with genuine warmth that I looked forward to hearing their Saturday stories soon.

When I got back home, I rented office space with the money I earned from my keynote speech. Every Day Is Saturday was now officially open for business. I sent an email message to all the conference attendees and offered them private training sessions. I got 200 of them to sign up for my Every Day Is Saturday coaching program. I called all those people and talked to them personally to get them on board with the program. Between the check I was given for speaking at the

Hawaii conference and the money I secured in future coaching sessions, I'd managed to amass $150,000 in the four short weeks since leaving that real estate course.

I had confidence before, but now it soared off the charts. This is where I was meant to be, doing what I needed to be doing. I'd come a long way, baby.

Chapter Eleven:

Back From the Past

Growing up in Bradford, PA I was faced with circumstances a whole lot different than those I would find in Cincinnati several decades later. I was faced with a lot of challenges during my childhood. Fortunately, I chose to embrace them rather than blame others, and I took full responsibility for my own destiny…eventually.

I know, I know. Sounds like a motivational pep talk, right? Face your fears instead of running from them. Embrace the challenge. But I'm here to tell you, I'm a real guy who did it. I managed to get past my past.

I grew up in the '70s, raised by a single mom as one of eight kids. Bradford is a little town about 80 miles south of Buffalo, New York, right on the state border. It was once a booming oil town, beginning in the 1870s and continuing until the 1940s, when the price of a barrel got too low to support the economy. The oil wells were left behind as the community moved to manufacturing to support its population.

The good news is that I grew up within the confines of such a small town where I had tons of support from everyone. But the bad news was that it was a small town and without a lot of entertainment options, it was easy to find trouble.

My dad stuck around until I was just a few months old before coming down with "the grass is greener" syndrome and split. Mom was 40-years-old at the time and since she already had a brood of seven to feed and care for, I'm pretty sure I was not a planned addition to the family. My older brother, Chris, was 17-years-old when I was born; a senior in high school. If you think about it, he was old enough to be my dad himself.

Since I never had a father around during my childhood, I didn't think it was strange to be in a one-parent household. I never really missed my dad because Mom was strong enough for both of them. My siblings all knew the man who'd fathered us and some of them thought he was just plain nuts. None of them, however, were huge fans after he left our mom to raise eight kids by herself. I guess I really didn't miss out on anything by not having him around.

I was a good athlete and played a lot of sports. I always sprinted onto the baseball field or basketball court and peered intently at the sea of faces in the audience but I never did see my Mom's among them. She just couldn't make it because she was always working. Fortunately, a lot of the other parents took me in and treated me as their surrogate son.

I always thought it would be nice to have a mom or dad present at my games. The idea of sitting down to a real dinner with my entire family was appealing, too. But none of that happened at my house. Dinner time was almost stressful; as the youngest of eight kids I had to eat really fast, especially if I wanted seconds; only those who finished eating first were privileged enough to take the last bit of food out of the pan. I guess that's where my "kill or be killed" mentality comes from today. My personality, especially my sense of humor, definitely comes from my mom, though. She was a sharp wit and a well read woman with a dry sense of humor that could catch you completely off guard.

A lot of people wonder what kind of home could house that many kids. It was a huge old house which saw its 100th birthday in the 1970s. It contained four bedrooms to sleep eight kids and a mom. There was no insulation in the place so it was very cold in the winter. All we had for warmth were gas heaters located throughout the house and they frequently blew out during the coldest months. When I turned eight-years-old, I gained the privilege of lighting those heaters by myself. I would retrieve a book of matches from the bathroom (the original air freshener), carefully light a match and hold it to the pilot flame. Whoosh! The heater would light with a bang and I'd throw the burnt match into the bottom. It's amazing that the whole house didn't go up in smoke from one of those old heaters malfunctioning.

That wasn't the only peculiarity of the house; most doors didn't have doorknobs. The guts of the doorknobs were still there, but there was no way to turn them so we used a butter knife or a wrench to get in and out.

Still, it was a great house to grow up in. When my brothers were home, we constantly played games, with backyard Nerf baseball as one of our favorites. There was always plenty of love to go around and Mom ran the show efficiently.

No one in town ever judged us. We actually had lots of friends, real friends, all of whom would show up for our annual New Year's Eve bash. We didn't have a lot and our home sure wasn't nice, but around the holidays we really did it up big. Although every year one sibling would head off to college or move for their career, they would always come home for Christmas.

The whole family loved playing Monopoly. I was obsessed with the game and even at the ripe old age of ten, decided I just had to collect every hotel and house on Baltic and Mediterranean. I knew exactly what properties sold for what price. This was my first experience in real estate and the first indication that I might enjoy buying and selling real properties later in life.

Bradford was a factory town whose biggest claim to fame was being the home of Case knives,

Kendall motor oil and Zippo lighters. Back in the 1970s and '80s, there was high demand for all three products, but especially those windproof Zippo lighters (there were a lot more smokers back then). Mom worked as a nurse at the Case knife factory. One of her coworkers, Ronnie, would come by each morning in a big van with a knife logo painted on the side to pick her up. The van would climb up the steep incline to our house and us kids would peer out the window, yelling to mom, "The knife's here!" Mom would come out of her bedroom dressed in her nurse's uniform and off she would go for an eight to 10-hour shift.

We kids got ready for the day in the bitter cold of that drafty house and then made our way to school on our own. I attended Saint Bernard's and I walked with my brother Jim until I was in the fourth grade, when I was deemed mature enough to make the walk alone.

There wasn't much to fear in Bradford, though. Everyone knew everyone else and all the adults watched out for the town's children. The neighborhood was full of kids. It only took one to grab a baseball glove, a mitt and a ball and knock on everyone else's door until we accumulated a full team. As we got older, we walked to Callahan Park to play basketball. We played sandlot baseball all day and played in the streets each night until the streetlights came on. That was a typical summer day in Bradford.

What really stands out about growing up there was my strong, supportive group of friends. I learned very early that it's important to surround yourself with good people. I've carried that through to my business today, too, but now I refer to my close acquaintances as a mastermind group. Back then I guess we had a "friends mastermind", we just didn't call it that.

I developed a stuttering problem about the time I was in second or third grade. I just couldn't speak very well. I stammered and I stuttered and with my name, the extent of the problem should be obvious. I'd get nervous anytime I had to call my best friend. As I dialed those last four digits, panic set in and I'd pray that Mike would answer the phone himself. But usually it was his mom. She'd ask who was calling and I had to say, "It's s...s...s...Sam." Sometimes I didn't even make it that far. I'd hang up as soon as I heard her voice, my hands dripping with sweat, because it took so much effort to get those two simple words out of my mouth.

My friends, however, at least my close friends, didn't make fun of my stuttering even though I often hopped on one leg to concentrate enough on the words I wanted to say in order to speak them clearly. I did get teased some, but nothing that scarred me for life.

I don't have a clue as to why I developed this problem when I did. All I knew is that I needed to figure out how to overcome it.

When I graduated eighth grade from Saint Bernard's, I had to go up to the altar and read a gospel scripture. I walked slowly down the aisle to the front of the chapel and stood behind the podium. The first thing I saw was my family, sitting in the front pew of the church in a neat, shiny row. They were leaning forward and holding their collective breath. I could tell what they were thinking. "How is he going to get any words out of his mouth? Will he be able to do this?" At the same I was praying, "Dear God, please let me get through this. Please help me read this scripture."

I wiped my sweaty palms on the front of my Sunday pants and opened my mouth to speak. There was a second of silence, then the first word came out just fine, and the ones after that, too. "Today I'll be reading from the gospel of John…"

My mother and brothers and sisters visibly breathed a big sigh of relief, sitting back as I continued to read the scripture. I got all the words out just fine.

The stuttering problem really pissed me off. I worked hard for years to get rid of it.

In the ninth grade I became friends with Mike A., whom I met at the public high school we both attended. Most of the deep friendships I formed during childhood survived many years of ups and downs.

Today Mike and I are still best friends. We are godparents of each other's children and served as best man in each other's wedding. Mike is the kind of rare friend who never judges and is always there for me. Even to this day, we can go months with no contact and with a single phone call pick right up where we left off, as if we just spoke yesterday. If you live long enough to have one Mike in your life, you are blessed.

Back then, times weren't so good; we grew up in an environment that was not conducive to becoming the next Bill Gates or George Clooney. My escape route led straight to my friends' houses; that's where I headed when times got really tough. This allowed me to dip a toe into the big pond of normal life where families with two parents sat down to dinner at the same time, and watched TV or played games together afterward.

I still use this as a way to de-stress today. I turn to my inner circle when I need a pick-me-up. I'm very loyal to my closest friends, as they are to me. We are always there for each other when it counts, no matter the miles between us.

Another close friend of mine was Mooney, aka my partner in crime. Bradford was a hunting town and the day after Thanksgiving school rooms were nearly empty because all the kids were out hunting with their parents. I didn't hunt or fish because I didn't have a dad to teach me those things.

But that doesn't mean I didn't make my own kind of fun. Mooney and I were fond of going into the woods behind my house with cans of hairspray and a Zippo lighter that belonged to his dad. Together those ingredients turned into instant blow torches – not so good for the flora, but very entertaining to a couple bored teenagers.

We were up to our usual antics one day, lighting a tree on fire, then putting it out – only this time the fire was too big. The tree went up in flames and they spread quickly through the dry branches and brush. Mooney and I sprinted away from the scene of the crime and the next thing we knew, a couple fire trucks were racing up the hill to extinguish the now out of control fire. Neighbors came out of their houses to watch the activity. "Oh my God! Do you see that fire on the hill?"

Mooney and I stupidly stood there along with the neighbors watching until the fire was completely put out. The firefighters coiled their hoses back up and tromped down the hill in their yellow coats and rubber boots, looking for witnesses. They questioned all of us, but particularly me and Mooney, who was working hard to keep his eyes wide and his expression innocent.

"Do you boys know anything about that fire?" We shook our heads but then the firefighter held out a Zippo lighter in the palm of his hand. "Is this your lighter? It says 'Mooney' on it." Unfortunately, the evidence didn't lie; that, of course, was my buddy's surname and it was undeniably his dad's lighter. The jig was up. Luckily, we got off with a stern warning. Sure, we could have blown up the whole town (remember all those abandoned oil fields in the area?) but we didn't and that was the fun of growing up in a small town where we could enjoy all sorts of harmless (used loosely) mischief.

When I got older, Mike A. and I would find someone of drinking age to go across the border to

New York and buy us a case of beer. We'd take our six pack up on the hill behind my house and drink it all down. If I was doing things like that today, I'd be put in juvie jail.

Then there was the party after a basketball game. It was hosted by a girl whose dad was in the naval academy. One of my buddies managed to find her dad's naval cap and plopped it on his head, then we left with him wearing the hat and carrying a beer. A local cop spotted us and tailed us as our car left the house. Later we found out that my buddy's parents were listening in on a scanner tuned to the police band and heard, "We're tracking the sailor. He's driving a white over brown Plymouth Volare…" It took them a minute before they realized what was going on. "Hey that's our car!"

Back then, those were the types of things we did for entertainment. It was all in good fun and we never hurt anyone else or ourselves.

Life was simple and things were pretty good even though Mom didn't ever seem to have enough money to go around. When I was in elementary school we survived on food stamps. I didn't see anything wrong with going to the A&P at the beginning of each month and handing over a wad of coupons to the cashier. We never had cash so I didn't know any different. Looking back on those times, I really have no idea how my mom made ends meet with eight kids to care for but one thing is certain: she knew how to stretch a buck until it nearly snapped. And she made sure we were all grateful for everything we did have instead of focusing on what we did without.

One year, right before Thanksgiving, Mom ordered a new stove. It was delivered the night before Thanksgiving, with all my brothers and sisters home from college for the holiday. There was a huge blizzard that night that dropped two feet of snow in less than four hours.

These poor guys from the appliance store were out in that weather with our new stove in the back of their van. We watched from the living room window as they pulled up into the driveway, excited about the new stove. Mom was going to love this! Just wait until she got home from work and saw it in the kitchen! It would be a happy Thanksgiving indeed! The deliverymen managed to get the range on a dolly and up the steps into our kitchen amidst the blowing winds and drifting snow.

As soon as Mom walked through the door several hours later after her shift, we greeted her with big smiles and ushered her right into the kitchen to admire her new stove. Mom, however, wasn't quite as excited as we were. "Where's the turkey?" We all looked at her with blank faces. "The turkey! There was a turkey in the old oven." What? You mean…

Sure enough. Dinner was going to be slim pickings unless we did something quick. Mom had us all pile into the car and headed to the junkyard so we could find our old stove and get our Thanksgiving turkey back. Heck, it's not like we could afford to get another one.

The nine of us squeezed into the big old boat Mom drove around town and we headed to the local scrap yard in snow so dense you could barely see your hand in front of your face let alone street signs through the windshield. All the while, Mom kept up a steady litany of "How could you let them take that stove with the Thanksgiving turkey in it?"

When we got to the junkyard, we all jumped out and headed different directions in search of our holiday dinner. We pulled stuff apart and climbed on top of old cars in the hunt for the old stove. Some long, frigid minutes later, one of my brothers shouted that he'd found it. He pulled out the roasting pan complete with pale-skinned bird, climbed back down off the scrap heap and we headed home to enjoy our Thanksgiving dinner the next day. How could we eat that turkey after it had spent hours in the junkyard? Waste not, want not, as my mother was fond of saying.

It really didn't matter that money was always in short supply during my younger years. My fondest memories are of the things we used to do together, not of the things we had.

After all the other kids left, it was just me and my next oldest brother at home with Mom. During the school year, Mom and I looked forward to Friday nights when we would lie on blankets on the floor and watch our favorite shows, *The Incredible Hulk* and Donny and Marie. Saturday nights it was *Fantasy Island* and *The Love Boat*. My older brother had his own friends and better things to do so it was just me and Mom spending time together. Those nights huddled in front of the TV were simple but special.

I remember Mom being tired a lot. She worked so hard to earn money but she proved she didn't need a husband. As a way to de-stress, it was common back then to tip the bottle each night. At one point Mom's drinking started to get out of hand and one of her friends convinced her to join Alcoholics Anonymous. In our small town there weren't a whole lot of places to hold the meetings and besides, Mom couldn't just leave me home alone at night so often the group ended up at our house. I had to be home during these meetings but it wasn't a big deal to me. Mom introduced me to everyone as they arrived, "Sam, I'd like you to meet Mary A. And over there is Tom W." Then I would go upstairs and watch TV on the old black and white set in the bedroom while Mom hosted the AA meeting downstairs.

After the meeting was over, Mom served coffee, tea and cookies and I was allowed to come back downstairs to join the crowd. I treated it like any other social engagement, except that I wasn't allowed to use anyone's last name (even though I knew them all – it was a small town, after all). I'd saunter into the living room and greet the participants, "Hi there, Juanita L. How are you?" We saw many of the same people at the grocery store and I'd always play it on the sly. "Hey Mom! Look over there, it's Dave P.!"

I was just happy Mom was getting help. When she was sober, my mother was nice and funny. Although she faced daily challenges, she dealt with them with as necessary and had a phenomenal attitude – as long as she wasn't drunk.

One night, when I was in the eighth grade, Mom had fallen asleep in her favorite chair in the living room, as usual. Upstairs in my bedroom, I thought I was dreaming when I heard her say,

"Sam…Jimmy…Sam…Jimmy." When her voice got louder, I realized it wasn't a dream; something was wrong. I raced downstairs and found Mom on the floor. She couldn't get up. I dialed nine-one-one but I didn't know what else to do until the ambulance came and took her away. That really scared me. Mom ended up in the hospital with a broken hip. Apparently she'd fallen asleep in her chair, and then fell off onto the floor. She wasn't in the best of health and her bones were brittle. That short fall was enough to break one of them.

For the next three months, my mother lived in a hospital bed installed in the living room. Even from that undignified position she still managed to run our family as smoothly as to be expected. I had a paper route at this time and I delivered my newspapers each day after school. Mom collected the money for me and helped me open my own savings account, then a checking account when I was a teenager. Mom showed me how to manage my money and make it last.

Around the holidays, while she was still bed-ridden, Mom got a pink slip from the factory. That meant we couldn't afford to have a nurse come check on her and the responsibility of caring for my mother fell on me. Each day I had to get her onto a makeshift bucket commode and then empty it. I would cream her feet, get her dressed and comb her hair. I brought her toast in the morning and made her dinner each night after my paper route. I knew it was my duty, as her son, to care for her while she was incapacitated and she was grateful. I was, too. While Mom viewed it as a special time, it really was a learning experience for me – I learned to be respectful towards women. Mom recognized this and realized that her son was growing into a young man, and she was proud.

Mom brought me up right. She made sure I would never even consider striking a woman and expected me to address those older than me as "Missus". She expected me to carry the Crowley banner high. She showed me that we didn't need money to have integrity.

Mom bounced back from this setback just as she always did. She got a job at a nursing pavilion at the hospital and was appointed head nurse. Throughout my high school years, that's where she worked. In my junior year, I actually got a job at the Bradford Hospital handing out trays of food and cleaning up after meals. I worked there every day after school and saw my mom on the floors where I was delivering meals.

Working together meant I couldn't get away with anything. When report cards came out, Mom would meet me right there at the entrance to the ward. "Sam, I got your report card. If you don't bring that grade up in English we'll have a lot to talk about at home."

She always made sure I was well fed. Mom made the evening meal before she left for work each day at three in the afternoon. She didn't get home until 11 that night, when I was already in bed, but she would get up early the next morning to take me to school. Sometimes her shift would run from 11 at night to seven the next morning but Mom still made sure she was up and ready to take me to school by nine.

Shortly after breaking her hip, I was playing basketball as a senior in high school. The game took place at the opponent's school. While I was watching the game following mine, one of the parents from Bradford flagged me down. "Sam! Your mom was hit by a car! Apparently she was carrying groceries into the parking lot and some guy came around the corner and hit her." My heart nearly stopped and my insides turned to ice as I considered the consequences.

The adult drove me to the hospital. Mom was lying on a gurney in the Emergency Room, banged up again, pale and shaken but still alive.

Shades of my 8th grade year! During my senior year of high school, Mom was once again ensconced in the living room in a hospital bed. At my last high school basketball game, it was senior night and all of us senior players were escorted to center court by their parents. My sister Kate had to escort me in Mom's stead.

I continued to play basketball and the games were all broadcast on the local radio station. There was always a personal comment during each game, a shout out to my mom, "Hello Mrs. Crowley!" I knew she was listening to the radio because she would brag to others about how proud she was of me.

You may wonder how I ever made anything of myself after growing up in poverty. I never ended up in jail but I sure did party hard – we all did. After I went to college, I'd come home for Christmas break and get together with my buddies. We'd compare notes about parties and ask each other if it was unusual that we could all drink so much beer? In fact, at college, Bradford kids were known as those who could really pound it down. Many of the other kids were experiencing their first taste of partying but not for me and my friends; drinking like fish was old hat.

I came back home after dropping out of college in my sophomore year. In between then and (almost) joining the army, my mom suffered a stroke and lost the use of the right side of her body. She spent the summer of 1988 in a rehab center in Erie, Pennsylvania, while I stayed at home alone. Since Mom worked so much during my childhood, I didn't mind; I was raised to be very self sufficient. I'd go visit Mom once a week in the rehab center. She couldn't walk and her speech was slurred. I guess it was God's plan that I'd had to care for her those two times previously because I was better able to cope with this.

My mother was incredibly strong. She wasn't perfect; that would be impossible. But she did the best she could with what she had, even though the cards were stacked against her. She never said "I love you". I'm sure it was difficult to be all warm and fuzzy between her upbringing and the never-ending list of things-to-do she had to accomplish. But she didn't have to say it; I knew she loved me because she showed me each and every day.

Would it have been great to have grown up in Ozzie and Harriet's house? Sure, but that wouldn't have made me the same person I am today. I learned at a young age that becoming an entrepreneur was the route to self sufficiency. I knew how to do my own laundry by the time I was in fifth grade and as a teenager I bought my own Moped to take on my paper route. The most money my mother ever made was $17,000; between that piddly income and welfare, she managed to raise eight kids, five of whom graduated college and one even went to an Ivy League school. She did a hell of a job with what little she had and provided an excellent money management example for me and my siblings.

When Catherine Crowley died in 1997 there were lines of people snaking out the doors of the funeral home. She was a courageous, funny, pragmatic woman and she is very, very missed. RIP, Mom, I love you.

Chapter Twelve:

Drinking Parties to Engagement Party

I love a challenge – whether it's a personal or professional test, they pique my curiosity and strengthen my conviction. Show me the impossible job or the one no one else wants and I'm all over it.

It wasn't just in high school and college that I honed my party skills. When I got that first telephone sales job after leaving college and moving back home, I was sent to a territory in a part of New York State that no one else wanted: Watertown. There's not a whole lot in Watertown other than a big army base and the country of

Canada just to the north. But the only way for a cocky, young 22-year-old, like myself, to get promoted to outside sales was volunteering to sell phone book ads in Watertown.

I was looking for any chance to be recognized by the powers that be so I could receive my first promotion and a nice financial bonus. I was up for anything. I volunteered for anything and everything – all the stuff no one else wanted to do. That way I secured my position with the company, and since I was far away from corporate headquarters, it was the perfect opportunity to party and mess around every day with no one the wiser.

So just two years after becoming a sales rep, I left Buffalo and moved up to Watertown to start work at a new division. That's where I, along with a Boston terrier named Petey, spent the winter of '92. Watertown is right on Lake Ontario and it gets downright icy in the winter; when the lake freezes over everyone hunkers down in abject misery to wait for the spring thaw. It didn't take a genius to figure out why no other inside sales reps wanted this job.

I earned a good income. Rent in Watertown was cheap and because I didn't have anywhere to spend my money, I put most of it in savings.

When the campaign ended in Watertown, the company added insult to my injury; I was next sent to Plattsburgh, along the Vermont border. Each Monday I would drop Petey off at the dog sitter's house, drive to Plattsburgh, check into the Holiday Inn, and sell phone book ads all week long. That is, I sold ads when I wasn't playing John Madden football or hockey on the Sega system in my hotel room.

Plattsburgh was like the Island of Misfit Toys. Me and a whole bunch of other road warriors, young and inexperienced or old and out to pasture, comprised the sales force in that part of the state. There was no cat to come in and check to see what us mice were up to, so a typical day was playing video games during the morning and heading to the bar late afternoon. Tuesday night, in particular, was one of our favorites at the bar. That was karaoke night and we could buy beers for a quarter. We'd drink 'til we were drunk, sing off key until two a.m., then wake up the next day and do a couple sales calls before settling in for a good game of Sega football.

When Friday rolled around, I would drive back home, pick up Petey from his babysitter and sit around the house by myself all weekend playing more video games. I know – pretty pathetic, huh?

Between the winter I'd spent in Watertown and the spring in Plattsburgh, I'd had enough of my pathetic life. In May I asked the company if I could use my get-out-of-jail-free card and return to Buffalo. The mother ship had left me off in some godforsaken strip of land in the middle of nowhere. I'd had one big party in the "dorm" of the Holiday Inn hotel but I was now ready to return to civilized society.

It's not like I had a lot of leverage with my supervisor. Not only did I and the rest of the misfits not sell many ads during this time, it was the worst campaign in the company's history. But that's what they got for sending us all up there without supervision (the sales manager was who supposed to babysit us became ill and never made it to Plattsburgh) and sentencing us to eight months of pain and torture.

Luckily, this represented a short term sacrifice for me and one that would shape my later behavior. I figured I could do anything for long term gain and I proved that, indeed, I could. Over the next 15 years, I would continue to volunteer to do this, go there and try that. I always raised my hand. I love being a maverick!

I was finally brought back to Buffalo and promoted to outside sales. By the time 1995 rolled around, I'd been with the company five years and I was 27-years-old. I had a lot of partying under my belt and a lot of money saved up.

I bought my first home around this time, becoming the only guy I knew at my age with a home of his own. I called the mortgage company on a dare from my buddy, never expecting to be granted credit. Then again, if you don't try, how do you know for sure what's possible? The guy at the mortgage company looked at my finances, met with me and a couple weeks later, gave me a loan. The house I bought was a couple thousand square feet with three bedrooms and two baths, which I bought for $87,000. Now that was living!

Growing up in Bradford, I'd lived in that drafty old house of my mom's until I left home. It sold for $4,000 some years back, when my oldest sister, Kate, bought a new one for her. When I showed my mom the house I'd bought, it was all about the shock and awe. I gave her the grand tour and she remarked later, "Even the house your sister bought me only cost $55,000!"

In my early twenties, life was good. I worked hard, made money, owned my own home, partied and made lots of good friends – something I do wherever I go. I would get up each morning, work until noon on outside sales – just long enough to make my quota – hit the golf course by one in the afternoon, go home and hang out or take a nap. Fridays found me hanging with my buddies at Jack's Place bar, located in a Buffalo suburb, and there we'd stay until last call. The place was like *Cheers*; I'd walk in and everyone would shout, "Sam!" Life was simple. I wasn't dating anyone. I was above average in terms of numbers and my sales never fell below the second quartile. I kept my nose clean at work and lived my life as I wanted.

The following year I received a piece of mail that no one ever wants to see in their mailbox: a letter from the Internal Revenue Service. I ripped open the envelope and scanned the contents. I was being audited for my 1994 tax return.

My first reaction was to panic. I'd taken an early withdrawal from my 401(k) retirement account as a loan for the down payment to purchase my home. Had I done something wrong? I quickly called my accountant, Bill, who calmed me down, assured me there would be no problem, and scheduled an appointment to see me on Friday.

I spent the rest of the week compiling all the information and receipts for my 1994 tax return. I had a hard time sleeping, I was so anxious to meet with Bill and find out what I was facing from the IRS.

When I walked through the front door of Bill's office Friday afternoon with visions of debtor's jail in my head, I stopped short. *Hold the phone...this is new. Who's that hot, blonde receptionist Bill's got working for him?*

I adjusted my tie, cocked an eyebrow and affected a deep, manly tone of voice. "Hey there. I'm Sam Crowley." *As if she'll recognize you, idiot!*

"You're here to see Bill?" She was all business and cool as a cucumber while I sweated buckets, hoping I wouldn't embarrass myself.

"Did you just start working here?"

"Yes. I'm Angela." She turned her back to me and started typing. *That was kind of rude.*

Bill opened the door of his office and ushered me and my box of receipts inside. "Hello, Sam. Now about this audit..."

Audit, schmaudit. "Who's that girl out there working for you?"

Bill tilted his head toward the door as he regarded me across the surface of his neat desk. "Her? That's Angela Cooper. But, Sam, forget about her. She's taken. She's got a boyfriend. Now about your audit…"

"How long has she had this boyfriend?" I was like a dog with a bone. I wasn't about to give up until Bill reminded me I was paying him by the hour and we needed to get started.

We went through the material in my box and when Bill was through I walked back into the reception area. Without being too obvious, I looked Angela up and down one last time and casually told her I'd see her later.

I walked back down the sidewalk lining the strip mall to my office, which was located just doors away. I sat down at my desk and all I could think about was Angela. Should I call her? Was it too soon? I'd never done that before; agonize over calling a girl and asking her for a date. Actually, all of my dates prior to this had been set up for me or casual meetings at a bar that weren't "real" dates. I picked up the phone and dialed Bill's office. I had no idea what I was doing but I did know I couldn't focus on work until I at least tried to make plans with Angela.

She answered the phone on the second ring.

"Hey! It's Sam Crowley!"

"Hang on," she said quickly. "I'll put you through to Bill."

"No, no! Don't do that!" I must have sounded like a maniac. "I want to talk to you. Do you want to go to the movies this weekend?"

"I have a boyfriend," Angela replied. After a heartbeat, she continued. "I don't want to cheat on him but I could break up with him tomorrow and we could go out on Saturday."

I liked her answer. I had to respect a girl who had that kind of morals. "Great! Then we're on for Sunday? How about we go to Niagara Falls for dinner and a movie? Five p.m.? Here's where I live…"

Unfortunately, I didn't get her phone number. But, no worries. I hung up the phone with a silly smile on my face. I turned to my buddy at the desk next to mine and bragged about my success. "Check this out! I've got a date with the receptionist from Bill's office!"

"The hot blonde? You have a date with her?" Bobby was incredulous. Apparently the news of the new, hot blonde receptionist just doors away had already made the rounds of the office.

"Yep! Yours truly has a date set up with her. How do you like me now?"

The next day I went golfing as usual but this time I couldn't pass up the opportunity to brag to all my buddies. I talked about nothing else the entire time on the golf course – Angela this, Angela that, and wasn't I a smooth operator? I was sure proud of myself. When we were done and headed to the bar, I got into my Infiniti G20, complete with car phone the size of a brick mounted to the console next to the stick shift. "Hey guys, let me check my voice mail."

I made a big deal about dialing into my voice mail. After rubbing it in all day that I had a date with the hot blonde, I was on a roll. Life wasn't just good, it was great. There was no stopping Sam Crowley now.

Sure enough, there was a message from Angela. "Hey Sam, this is Angela Cooper. Listen, I gotta cancel tomorrow. My nephew is having a birthday party and I've got to go to that. Let's try to get together some other time."

My heart jumped down into my feet. I was mortified. My buddies started howling with laughter. "A nephew's birthday party? Dude, you just got the major blow off. You're such a loser!"

The rest of the night at the bar I got beat up pretty badly by my friends but, of course, I deserved it after all that chest pounding I'd done earlier.

I woke up Sunday morning nursing a hangover and headed to the phone. This was 1996 and caller ID was something you had to pay extra for but I'd bought one from Radio Shack a few months earlier. There was no way to block your number back then and I easily retrieved Angela's phone number. I just couldn't believe she'd canceled on me with such a lame excuse.

I didn't have anything to lose at this point so I called her at home. "Angela! Hey, it's Sam Crowley."

Silence. Then, "How did you get my number? Are you a stalker?"

"No, no, not me. I've got caller ID. You called, and your number came up on the screen."

"What do you do for a living? Are you a private investigator?"

"No, no. Listen, I thought you were going to your nephew's birthday party today."

Silence again. It lasted for a few seconds before Angela replied, "Oh yeah…I wasn't feeling well."

"Then let's go to the movies. Why don't you come over?"

After a half-hearted protest, she finally agreed.

When she showed up, the connection between us was both instant and powerful. Our personalities just clicked perfectly. It was a match made in heaven.

We drove to Niagara and saw *Mission Impossible* in the theater. I drove home after the movie and parked in front of my house. I didn't want her to leave. I opened the door on her side of the car and took her hand, drawing her out into the puddle of streetlight shining on the sidewalk. I kissed her right there, long and deep, tasting the strawberry sweetness of her lips.

That was it. It was all over. We went out every night for the next 10 days and got engaged a couple months later.

Sure, it wasn't an ideal start – I'd had to convince Angela to take a chance – but our relationship was meant to be. It was a God thing. And I thank Him every day for bringing me the woman of my dreams. And thank you, Angela, for putting up with all my foibles and fancies. Bet you didn't know what you were getting yourself into all those years ago sitting with me in the movie theatre watching Tom Cruise hang from the ceiling, eh?

Chapter Thirteen:

The Permanency of Death

Life is so fragile. We can have everything we've ever desired one minute, then lose it all the next and be given the chance to regain it, at least in regards to tangible things. Death, however, is permanent. And at some point in our lives, we come to the realization of just how short life really is; at some point we look in the mirror and face our own mortality.

When that happened to me, I also realized that it was time for me to become great at what I was doing. I wanted to squeeze every last little bit of toothpaste out of the tube of life. Life is too short for regrets and I'm going down swinging.

I got married to Angela largely because I didn't know if I would get hit by a bus or get cancer tomorrow. If the worst happened, I wanted to at least believe I'd given life every bit of effort I could.

But I didn't always deal with tragedy in such a positive manner. In fact, I needed to go off the deep end before I could swim back into the safe, shallow end of the pool. At some point I had to grow up, and this is how it happened.

It was 1997, almost a year since Angela and I had gotten engaged. My birthday is June 29th and that year Mom wanted me to come back to Bradford and hang out with my sister at her house. My sister's birthday is two days before mine, so we planned on celebrating both of our special days that Fourth of July weekend.

That's exactly what we did for my 29th birthday. Angela came with me so Mom and Sue could help with the planning of the wedding.

We were thinking about having the ceremony in Bradford since Mom wasn't getting around too good.

After a big meal and a slice of birthday cake, Mom gave me a check as she always did, in the amount of one dollar for every year of my age. I thanked her and tucked it into my wallet.

I played golf with my buddies at a course close to Bradford and Saturday night Angela and I went out for a while. When we returned, Mom was still up. She wanted to talk to Angela and they stayed up chatting for hours that night. Mom played the part of a perfect hostess. She was in a good mood, seemingly without a worry in the world, and a real chatterbox. Although she was in bad health, which often made her wake up on the wrong side of the bed, this weekend she was at peace and not the least bit cranky.

Before leaving Mom's house, Angela and I gave her a big hug and said goodbye on

Sunday, July sixth. We drove back to Buffalo and I mentioned to Angela how unusual it was for Mom to be in such a great mood with all the aches and pains she was experiencing. Although it had been a pleasant weekend, it was also kind of weird.

That Monday I was back at work. I had three sales calls to make, one scheduled at 10 a.m., another an hour later and a final call at noon. In between the first and second appointments, I experienced severe depression. I felt a heavy weight on my shoulders and a bowling ball rolling around in my stomach. Something was terribly wrong. Although I don't believe in mediums or psychic ability, I just knew that my mom had died. Visions of her life went through my mind, like a sad movie with my mother in the lead role. On my way to my eleven o'clock meeting, the weight of sadness became so heavy that I pulled over to the side of the highway and started crying. *What's wrong with*

me? Am I losing my mind? I better make a doctor's
appointment...

After my last sales call of the day, I drove
to my office. It wasn't actually an office, more of
an open space with a bunch of desks for all the
sales reps. I picked up my phone and pressed the
blinking message button. Three messages were
indicated by dit-dit-dit bleeps of the light.

The first message was from my oldest
sister, Kate, an attorney in New York. "Just wanted
to let you know that Mom died. Chris found her.
He went over to her house today and found her
dead in the living room. She was watching TV and
had a cigarette in her hand, burned down to her
fingertips. When I spoke with my sister Sue at the
funeral, she said she had the exact same feeling
after leaving mom's house that Sunday. She said
she pulled over on her way back to Boston and
cried, too.

It gave me chills to think my sister had experienced the same thing I did – a vision of Mom dying. No one in my family had ever had feelings like that before. It was bizarre.

Kate continued, "I called Chris and asked him to drive to Mom's house and check on her. He called me back and said, 'I'm sitting in the living room and she's dead'." Apparently Chris closed her eyelids, dialed nine-one-one, and then stuck around until paramedics arrived to whisk her body away.

As my mother's life came to an end, so did mine. The "old" Sam, the one who relied on his mother for strength and support, the one who didn't need to grow up, ceased to exist.

After listening to that message, I gently put the phone back in its cradle. The life was sucked right out of me, my very breath stolen from my mouth. I couldn't seem to move or to speak... someone asked me for a paper clip from my desk drawer or something inconsequential like that. What I heard was that Charlie Brown teacher voice again, "Blah, blah, blah, blah, blah, blah." My brain couldn't even process the words.

My mother was my everything. She was my rock. Growing up without a dad, she was only the parent I'd ever known. Having to go on without her…I couldn't comprehend how I was going to accomplish that.

Finally, I managed to get my butt out of that desk chair. I ran into my manager's office and yelled, "My mom is dead!" I then ran into the division manager's office and yelled, "My mom is dead!"

I was acting insane. I fled the office and got into my car. The managers ran after me, asking me where I was going. I didn't answer, but pressed my foot to the accelerator and gunned it back home.

Along the way I called Angela and gave her the news. "Remember, I told you how weird Mom was acting over the weekend? That was it – she was dying. Then I felt it earlier today. I don't know why but I felt like I was possessed or something."

When I arrived at home, Angela and I packed a couple bags and then headed to Bradford. I was driving like a mad man, doing 85 miles an hour. A state trooper pulled me over and that made me angry. Didn't he know I was on a mission? "My mom just died and I don't know what I'm doing with my life." Although it sounded crazy, the state trooper told me he was sorry for my loss and let me off with a warning.

When I got to Bradford, I found the whole family together again for the first time in 20 years. It was fun to have everyone gathered again that today, just like old times when we would play games during the holidays. But it was also sad. Our family was missing its central figurehead.

Like any traditional Irish Catholic family, we broke out the booze, had people over and told story after story about Mom. We laughed and we cried and we sat around with our heads in our hands wondering what we were going to do now.

The funeral came much too quickly. I rode along in the limousine to the cemetery, thinking, "This is it. This is really it. No more Mom." The day before we'd had a viewing at the funeral home. I was glad I'd seen her in person just a few days earlier; my brothers and sisters hadn't had that opportunity to spend time with her. I looked at her waxen face, so peaceful amidst folds of snowy white satin, and lost it. "You're in a coffin! How did this happen?" I wailed and I wept. I thought about watching *The Donny and Marie Show* and *Fantasy Island*. It seemed like just yesterday. I knew I was making a scene in the funeral home but I couldn't control myself.

The entire town showed up at her funeral, all the rich people and the poor ones, too, the people she used to work with at the factory and personnel from the hospital. Doctors, lawyers, blue collar workers – they all stood in line next to each other to pay their respects. Even without money, notoriety or an official title, she'd managed to influence so many. My mother brought together the entire town of Bradford. It was her final way of demonstrating that you don't need fame or fortune to positively influence others.

After the service, Angela and I drove back to Buffalo. I was numb and I wanted to stay that way so I started drinking, a lot. I was sinking in to a deep depression and becoming mean. I purposely picked fights with Angela. Any time she expressed dissatisfaction with something, anything, I would viciously bite at her, "What do you have to complain about? Your mom isn't dead."

Deep down inside I knew how silly and childish I was behaving. To avoid further conflict, I left. I just split. I called off the engagement.

I tried to bury myself in my job. I was working a campaign at a location an hour away and that was fortunate because I didn't want to be around Angela. I was a powder keg just looking for a match to set me off again. Monday through Friday I was out of town; on weekends I went back to Bradford rather than return to the home Angela and I shared in Buffalo.

Angela didn't know how to reach me and she didn't know what else to do so she found an apartment to rent. She packed up all of her belongings into boxes, all those familiar things that scented and decorated and graced our home, all gone into the dark confines of a box.

She tried one last time to reach me. The day before her appointment to sign the lease on her new apartment, she called me. "Sam, are you sure this is what you want?"

Just the sound of her voice on the other end of the line, with its caring, compassionate tone was enough to break through the barrier around my heart. I could keep it together as long as I was the Lone Ranger, untouched by anyone else's concern. But the minute I heard that familiar voice belonging to the woman I loved, I lost it. I glanced at the glass of whiskey in my hand and did my best not to sob but my words came out as an emotional stutter anyway. "No…no. I don't. Angela, please come back."

It was time to get back to my life. It had been two months since Mom had died. I'd needed the time to manage that information, to deal with it. In the process, I'd become an alcoholic. Now it was time to grow up and give it up. And with Angela back at my side where she belonged, lending me her love and support, I could do it.

The following month I got a call from my division manager saying the company wanted to move me to Cincinnati, Ohio, to become a senior account executive. The promotion meant a higher salary and more responsibility. I realized that with Mom gone, I had no more ties to western Pennsylvania. Why not?

I told Angela I wanted to make the move. It was time to change my life. I wanted to start working like I desired success. "I'm going to do something great in Cincinnati. I'm going to dedicate my life to my job." I owed it to my mom. Although she'd always been proud of me, she knew I'd never used all of my God-given talents, I knew that I was holding back due to the immaturity that made me focus on my selfish desires instead of what I could accomplish if I just put my heart and soul into it.

The company relocated me on their dime and it was just the break I needed. I could start a whole new life in a place where no one knew the old Sam, the drinker and partier extraordinaire. Nobody knew that guy. It was like being in the witness protection program. In a fresh new location I could be whoever I wanted to be, reinvent myself.

It was Halloween day when Angela and I made the long haul from Buffalo to Cincinnati. We bought the house of dreams, big enough to accommodate a growing family. I started working like I meant it, getting in the office at five each morning, working hard, and becoming the top sales rep in the entire country. It wasn't long before I began earning $100,000. I was putting in the effort and seeing the results. I finally had things right in my mind and it allowed me to accomplish more than I'd ever thought possible.

At this time I was still basically single and I still liked to party. But on February 28, 1998, I had a whim to get married and that's what I did. All the planning we'd done for our big wedding was shot; Angela and I just flew our close family members to Cincinnati and eloped with the 20 people who had showed up that Saturday night. Later we had a nice reception so the rest of the family could celebrate with us.

When you think about the frailty of life and the finality of death, you begin to realize you can do anything you want to do – within reason, of course. You can't be a brain surgeon without putting in the learning time, of course. Within your craft, within the definition of your Saturday, however, you can be the best ever if only you make the decision to do it.

I made the decision to no longer be the life of the party, the guy who golfed and took naps every day. That wasn't important anymore. As I approached the age of 30, I decided to make something out of my life.

This transition to maturity had been building up inside me for some time. Although I had earned a good reputation in the office, I wasn't an elite salesperson – and that's what I wanted to be. I wanted to people in the company to say my name and associate it with the very best.

Over the course of the next couple years, I was flown to the Bahamas, Las Vegas and Puerto Rico on all-expense paid awards trip I had earned by becoming the top sales manager in the company, month after month. And it all happened after one simple decision to not settle for being just average. I didn't want to be the class clown all my life. I wanted to be respected. Now that my mom was deceased, I decided it was time to grow up and be the man she also knew I could be. There were all sorts of opportunities in front of me, if only I would embrace them.

Every now and then I pull out my wallet and extract that check Mom wrote to me for 29 dollars. I've always kept it as a reminder of her. It has her writing and it smells like her, even after all these years. It's a good memory.

CHAPTER FOURTEEN:

MAKING EVERY DAY A SATURDAY

Turning every day of my life into Saturday didn't happen overnight – even after I got that great gig in Hawaii. When I got home, I was still just Sam Crowley, dad and would-be motivational speaker. But I was almost there, almost doing every day what I used to reserve only for Saturdays when I worked in the corporate world.

It was time to get serious about building my dream. I didn't feel as if I really had a business when I was working from home, so I rented a small office space with not much more than a desk and a laptop from one of those places that provides a shared receptionist, conference room, and other business accoutrements. Away from home I could get into the mindset of a professional speaker, trainer and seminar leader.

I am a firm believer in the power of networking; someone once told me that "your network creates your net worth" and I live by that. So I made it a point to stop in and chat with my office neighbors on a regular basis. You never know when someone is going to be that missing link in your organization. You could be only one contact away from exploding your life – but if you never take the time to stop and say hello, that opportunity will forever remain lost.

At the beginning of September in 2008, a couple young guns moved into the office directly across the hall from mine. Shortly after they got settled in, I poked my head inside their open door. Two heads, one brunette and one auburn, were bent over their desks, faces focused intently on the screens of their laptops. "Hey! How are you doing? I'm Sam Crowley. What do you guys do?"

"We're investment bankers," answered the auburn-haired one with a firm handshake and a ready smile. "We handle financial affairs for clients, buy stocks online and things like that."

They introduced themselves as Ben and Charles. As we continued to talk, I felt very comfortable with them, finding that we had a lot in common. Charles had studied at Penn State and he had the gift of gab, much the same as me. Ben was quieter and much more focused. Both Charles and Ben had left well paying jobs as asset managers at a bank after being bit by the entrepreneurial bug. They decided to pool their resources and name their newly formed company GF Financial.

When it was my turn to share, I told the pair about Every Day Is Saturday. They thought it was a great name for a business like mine. And Charles and Ben were on the same quest I was – trying to make every day they spent in the office feel like a Saturday.

As time wore on, I found myself spending more and more time with Ben and Charles. Ben, in particular, became a very close friend and confidante. He wanted to know what I was working on and I explained that I was developing my first product, which I would name Six Days To Saturday. I knew I wanted to present a lesson for each day of the week but I wasn't quite sure how to get there. I thought there could be a CD named Monday with a lesson plan about breaking free from drudgery, another CD named Tuesday with its own lesson, etc.

Ben and Charles were intelligent, savvy and entrepreneurs just like me. I trusted their opinions. The three of us spent a lot of time in the GF Financial office, marking up their whiteboard with ideas; it became the mastermind board for my Six Days To Saturday info product.

With the help of my mastermind group (who says it needs to be large? As long as you've

THE JOURNEY TO MAKING EVERY DAY A SATURDAY   269

got one or two people you trust and respect, you've got yourself a mastermind!), I decided to record an infomercial that would run 24/7 on the radio. Ben and Charles agreed to fund my business growth through GF Financial venture capitalists. Charles hit the phones and set up meetings. Through his network he got the name and number of a direct response marketing company that I contacted. It was my intention to contract the company to handle my infomercial using $300,000 of the funds my new joint venture partners were working on raising to buy radio spots and produce the product.

Ben prepared a pro forma. In return for the investment funding, I ceded 50 percent of my company over to Ben and Charles.

The marketing company was a great choice. It was located in Minnesota and they had a lot of experience working with many big companies. As soon as I told them about my Six Days To Saturday product idea, they totally got it; in fact, they suggested I put together a workbook to accompany the CDs. Together we decided that the sweet spot, price wise, was $299 and for that price, buyers were entitled to get a free item, which would be a bonus Every Day Is Saturday CD.

Because the marketing company owned inventory at radio stations, serving a hundred markets around the country, they promised my infomercial would reach literally millions of potential clients.

Before I knew it, everything I'd accomplished since returning from my first big speaking gig in Hawaii would soon turn my little business into a multi-million dollar enterprise!

It was time to get things settled properly with Ben and Charles so we put together a new business agreement and went full steam ahead. Each day the stock market closed at four p.m. and that's when the three of us would gather and flesh out further ideas for Every Day Is Saturday. The whiteboard in their office got a lot of use and we spent weeks on laborious work and research in between investor meetings, graph preparation, logo creation, etc. We settled on the details of the final Six Days To Saturday product: Monday – *Feeling the Pain*; Tuesday – *Preparing for Success*; Wednesday – *Taking Action*; Thursday – *The Winds of Adversity*; Friday – *The Power of Commitment*; and finally, Saturday – *You Are a Champion*, the first day of waking up and doing what you love for a living.

By the middle of September, 2008, the stock market started to tank. Obviously, being in the investment banking business and managing funds for their clients, this greatly affected Ben and Charles and, in fact, greatly distracted them. The Dow Jones Industrial Average (DJIA) was falling steadily each day by 600 points. It became too difficult for Charles to focus on more than one crisis at a time and he dropped out of Every Day

Is Saturday to focus full time on appeasing and advising clients of GF Financial.

That left just me and Ben. Although we'd only known each other little more than a month, it felt as if we were lifelong friends. During this very difficult period, I'd pop into his office and observe him watching the numbers flashing across his computer with a look of anguish on his face. As soon as he saw me, he would close the lid to his laptop and put his head in his hands. Our time together was a brief respite for Ben, who was being subject to a relentless pounding from his clientele. When the DJIA fell to 7,500 points overnight, he lost hundreds of thousands of dollars for his clients.

It was horrible timing for Six Day to Saturday, too. We never raised the $300,000 needed to move forward with the infomercial project. The market crashed at the same time we were courting investors. While I felt sorry for Ben, I had to move forward with my business.

Now that we had the content fleshed out, my job was to get into the recording studio and produce the actual product. Recording studio time is expensive; I was getting bids that started at $500 per hour. I came up with an idea to get around this obstacle – using the sound room at my church! I recorded the first audio presentation Monday.

I played it back that afternoon. It was bad. Really bad.

Although it wasn't the first time I'd recorded something, I just couldn't seem to translate my passion for the product to the actual recorded message. Ben, ever blunt, listened to the recording and commented, "We're putting our money behind this crap?" I welcomed this gift of feedback; in fact, I considered him a real asset to the company because of his ability to pinpoint what needed to change. Ben told me in no uncertain terms that I needed to go back to church and record it again.

The second time was much better and after that, I got into the rhythm and flow. It took me a week to finish creating each day's CD for Six Days To Saturday, ending just before Thanksgiving.

I was ready to launch. The problem was that the market had officially crashed; the country was facing a recession. There were no investors willing to trust our product or fund the company's progress. We had one foot on the grave, the other on a banana peel. Ben had gone through the entire process with me and he now found himself living the Every Day Is Saturday program by necessity.

As the end of the year approached and Christmas loomed on the horizon, the Minnesota marketing company was pushing us to launch the product. They were no longer so keen on getting the Every Day Is Saturday message out. After all that time over the last three months creating the content, putting in everything we had to give, amassing inventory, now the direct response marketing company was getting cold feet. The pro forma Ben had developed earlier would no longer work in this new, downturned economy; the numbers just weren't there anymore. The Minnesota company backed out of the project, giving us a polite "No thank you" after it became obvious the market was shifting.

In the midst of this kink, along comes another set of property manager woes. The Christian guy, Robert, whom I hired before leaving Bradford to manage my rentals, was giving me the run around. I checked in with him the first week of December but he dodged my questions. I didn't really want to know what was happening, but I called a handful of tenants anyway. Apparently they'd been paying rent but Robert wasn't recording it or depositing the funds.

Conveniently after that, Robert started dodging my calls. He wouldn't answer his cell phone and his wife wouldn't call me back, either.

Thanks a lot, buddy. You've just ruined my Christmas.

Over the holiday I stewed in my own juices, knowing I would have to return to Bradford to clean up the mess over there. The day after Christmas I drove back. Robert was nowhere to be found; he'd vacated his apartment and stole all my cash. All in all, he took me for about $7,000.

Once again, the problem was my fault. Although I didn't want to micromanage anyone, I just didn't pay enough attention to what was going on. I was much more focused on Every Day Is Saturday than I was on the rental management process.

Out of the four or so property managers who had a go at working for me in the year and a half prior, Robert's dishonesty was the worst. Robert had brought God into the equation, used Him as leverage to get the job. What self-respecting Christian would stoop that low?

I ended up staying in Bradford until New Year's Eve. One of my tenants, Dennis, who was unemployed at the time, saw my dilemma and took pity on me. It was almost more than I could take: the Six Days To Saturday failure to launch, the marketing company pulling out of the deal, the "Christian" property manager who had ripped me off. Dennis was a good guy. He told me to go back to Cincinnati to enjoy the rest of the holiday while he collected rent and fixed things up. In fact, Dennis jumped into the position with both feet; he was a real Godsend in my life at that time.

I drove back to Cincinnati on New Year's Eve in the middle of a huge snowstorm. I was finding it hard to regain a positive outlook. As I drove, I replayed all the things wrong in my life. I was losing money and I couldn't seem to get my company off the ground, I couldn't find the right person to manage my rentals, I was away from my family... I reached a hand to the console of my car to grab a drink of water…and hit a patch of black ice. I did a 360 across the freeway, spinning right in front of a semi truck, then crossing into the lanes of traffic going the opposite direction. My car slid backward across the ice and landed trunk first in a ditch. The engine stalled and snow continued to pound down on the windshield, obliterating everything in sight.

I sat there, totally pissed off, feeling like Ebenezer Scrooge before being visited by the Ghost of Christmas Past. For all intents and purposes, I had completely missed the holidays this year. *Why didn't that semi just run me over?* That would have solved all my problems.

Eventually, I grabbed my cell phone and dialed 911. I asked the operator to send a tow truck to my location. While I was waiting, a policeman came by, knocked on the window, and asked if I was all right. *Just peachy, Officer.*

I got out of the car when the tow truck arrived to pull it out of the ditch. The left wheel was cockeyed, which wasn't a good sign, but the tow truck driver assured me I could drive it if I didn't go over 50 miles an hour. What choice did I have? All I wanted to do was get back home and I didn't really feel like going the *Planes, Trains and Automobiles* route.

He wasn't kidding. As I got back on the freeway and headed once again toward home, I tried getting the car up to 65 miles an hour but it shook and rattled so bad I thought I was entering the atmosphere. Needless to say, it took a long time to get home.

Things have to look up...right?

Meanwhile, back at the office, I focused on getting my first product off the ground. Charles and I had a falling out over a major issue and I felt uncomfortable with him remaining as a partner in my business. Ben and I worked it so we could buy Charles out, Ben using his credit card to cover some of what he owed Charles in hopes of getting paid back before the bill came due.

It was also at this time that Ben and I agreed to go our separate ways. There had been too many distractions in the few months we worked together and the synergy just wasn't there any longer. Ben and I had formed a friendship but both agreed I would be better off alone with my product launch. Ben gave me his blessing and thanked me for bringing him along for the ride. I will always be grateful for Ben, without whom there would have never been a Six Days To Saturday product. I could see he was falling on really hard times. I wrote Ben a check for his third of the business so I could get 100 percent ownership back, then visited a lawyer to draw up the paperwork and make it legal.

Now I was on my own again and if anything was going to happen with Every Day Is Saturday, it was up to me to make it so. However, I had no sales page, no website to sell the product, no database to email – nothing.

Spring came to Cincinnati and I still didn't have a product launch. The good news was that Dennis was doing a great job managing the properties in Bradford and I had money coming into my bank account again. I never heard from Robert again, but I did hear many more stories from others about how much that guy took from me.

In order to move forward, I needed some help and I decided to begin searching for joint venture (JV) partners who could help me launch my product. Everyone who has a product to launch online – whether that's one item or a 1,000 – needs a JV partner. The art of the deal in a JV is two people coming together to create a win-win situation where both parties profit. I was looking for people who could promote my product to their mailing list and in return receive a 50 percent commission on every sale.

I tried to crack the JV code myself, but I felt awkward asking people I barely knew to send an email for me. That's when I decided to contact a JV broker, someone who gets paid to connect two people: a person with a product and a person with a mailing list. The broker gets a percentage of the deal just for making the connection. Most of the brokers I got in touch with wanted $10,000 upfront and that was out of my budget. So I contacted Sean, who was referred to me by an acquaintance. Sean had prior dealings with people in the personal development industry and he only wanted 10 percent of gross sales so he was a perfect fit.

I was still lacking a few things before my product launch could happen: good sales copy, a merchant account, and the finished product. Sean started making all that happen. He quickly got people lined up to take care of everything and that's when I realized it was finally, really going to happen. My product launch would become a reality at last!

I pushed myself into high gear, working night and day on sales copy, auto responder sequences and all the other little details that would make the product launch flow perfectly. I was shooting for a launch date of April 21, 2009. Sean almost single-handedly made it happen. He made sure I had all my ducks in a row by calling me each morning and every evening, ensuring that I was working on the right things at the right time.

Before the official launch date, Sean had me record a series of videos educating people about who I was and what Every Day Is Saturday was all about (a "pre-launch"). Sean provided social proof in the form of getting me on TV. In return for accessing the video content online, an opt-in box required names and email addresses that I could re-use later to send notice that Six Days To Saturday was available for sale.

April 21st finally arrived. The product launch email went out instantly from a hundred JV partners that Sean had set up. As the day progressed, I got email after email popping up in my inbox with the message line, "new sale". Not only did every one of those emails represent money in my pocket, it allowed me to build a huge database. My list went from a few hundred people to over 10,000 in a single day!

This was it – exactly what I wanted to see happen. People came to my sales page at the front end, receiving the Six Days To Saturday CD program at no charge except shipping and handling costs, no matter where the product was being mailed. In return for the free product, each person was automatically signed up for membership in an online community where they could access new CDs, live webinars, and classes for $97 per month.

This is what is referred to as "forced continuity" – gaining permission to charge buyers monthly for new products or services. At the end of the day we got well over 200 people signed up to pay $97 per month, or about $20,000 a month income.

I was giddy with success!

After this initial triumph, I worked on fine tuning the process. That summer I flew to San Diego to meet with several large affiliates who could further spread the word about Every Day Is Saturday and the Six Days To Saturday product.

I scheduled a re-launch of the product for August. This was my opportunity to take everything we'd done wrong the first time and perfect it. This time I had a thousand affiliates sending out the product email. More and more people were entering my sales funnel and I offered both upsells and cross sells. Another thousand people signed up for the continuity program which brought in another $100,000 a month – practically out of thin air!

You *can* think and grow rich. You can create something out of nothing. Create intellectual property and find a place for it. That's what I did. I just spoke into a microphone for six hours, told my story, asked people to feel their pain in order to recognize the problems they needed to overcome. In return for telling my story and using the power of networking, I created a path to income of $100,000 per month.

As of September, 2009, when most people were complaining about the economy, I had a $1,000,000 business. Each year I rewind to this time to remind myself that I can truly accomplish anything. I remember how I'd once filed bankruptcy and went back to working in a cubicle. I'm thankful to say, my life no longer looks anything like that.

As long as you stay in the game, you will always find a market for your product – you just have to keep moving forward.

After that big product launch, it attracted the attention of a multitude of people. Now I'm getting calls from others who want access to my database, which numbered 70,000 after that August re-launch.

Almost overnight, I became somebody in the personal development industry. I didn't intend to become a guru; all I wanted to do was get my message out and help others. But after this big success I started getting invitations to speak in person and via phone events, as well as being invited to present at various boot camps featuring some really big names.

At the end of 2009, I looked back on the amazing journey of the previous year. I sent Ben a copy of the Six Days To Saturday program along with a heartfelt thank you card. He had as much to do with my success as I did. And I continually remind myself that had I not extended my hand that day back in September of 2008 to Ben, if I hadn't introduced myself, if I hadn't been passionate about the power of networking, my Six Days To Saturday program would never have been created.

People can innately sense your energy and if you have lots of positive energy flowing, they want to be in on whatever you're creating. Instead of focusing on the challenges I'd faced in the past, I talked to Ben about where I was going in the future and that's the message that resonated with him.

Although Ben's infomercial idea didn't pan out, the product launch became much better after I connected with my JV. I ended up getting more revenue – and a whole lot of ancillary publicity. After the re-launch, I was asked to appear on a Fox News program in New York City. There I was, heading down Avenue of the Americas toward the big Fox News building. I was Sam the Class

Clown, Sam the Sales Rep, Sam the Division Manager – all of those things yet none of them anymore, sitting on the set of a major television program, describing what it meant for every day to be Saturday. After that appearance, I was also featured in a Cincinnati newspaper.

I'd finally made it – I was somebody.

Yet, I was still the same person I'd always been. I was still husband to Angela and father to Madeline, Laura and Paige. I still took them to school and treated them to ice cream every now and then. Every day was, indeed, a Saturday for Madeline – and me – at last.

CHAPTER FIFTEEN:

A REASON FOR EVERYTHING

Just when you think it's safe to go back into the woods is when you're most likely to become the victim of a bear attack. I've seen it happen over and over again. Yet, upon reflecting on those times in my life when God threw a big wrench in the works, I realize that everything really does happen for a reason.

After Every Day Is Saturday really took off, I was faced with property manager woes yet again. Dennis didn't rip me off, but he did let me know he was tired of managing and maintaining the properties in Bradford. It was a lot of work and he'd done a great job for me; he was entitled to a break. The problem was that this left me with a big decision yet again. Once again Angela and I had to decide whether or not we should relocate.

I had learned a few things over my first stint as landlord. I knew I could make it work, but I needed to be smarter. This time I decided it would be wise to find a house outside of Bradford proper, so we wouldn't be living right down the street from our tenants. Sure, they were nice people but it was a little too convenient for them to hunt me down every time a faucet started leaking or a driveway needed shoveling.

I began looking online for properties, in February of 2010, and found a Victorian house with magnificent architecture in Springville, New York, smack dab in the middle between Buffalo and Bradford. It was the childhood home of Glenn "Pop" Warner, famous football coach and founder of the self-named organization for young athletes; however, it was also beaten up and broken down.

I thought it was perfect; Angela, however, was skeptical – and resistant.

"Honey," I wheedled, "Do you have one more remodeling job in you?"

With memories of using the bathtub as a dishwasher, she shook her head adamantly. "I love the house we have right now!"

I managed to convince Angela moving was the right decision since we'd lost our property manager and the person overseeing the rentals was only doing so on a temporary basis. "But don't worry, Honey," I consoled Angela. "There won't be any tenants showing up at our door this time."

By April the Crowley family was moving yet again. Luckily, I managed to get our house in Cincinnati rented before we pulled up stakes and set out for New York State. I put an ad on Craigslist and by the second week of March, I had renters all lined up; a nice, young family just starting out and relocating from Atlanta, Georgia. Their situation really struck a chord with me, reminding me of my own little family back when I worked in the corporate world. I've heard horror stories of using Craigslist to find tenants but once again, dismissed what the masses had to say and used my own intuition. I could not have found a better family if I tried. And the bonus was that I saved thousands in property management fees by doing it myself.

So off to Springville we went, our family following the moving van across the state line.

I'll never forget the look on Angela's face as she viewed our new house for the first time. It hadn't been occupied for 18 months and a tree had fallen in on the front entrance. Standing inside with the kids, Angela looked about her and shook her head in disbelief – and perhaps even utter despair. It was a disaster; utterly disgusting. The house had been built in the 1870s of plaster and lath and never updated within the last century, from the looks of it. The radiators were blown out and cracked due to the extreme cold. But I'd gotten it cheap – it was valued at $125,000 and I picked it up for $75,000.

We didn't have anywhere else to live while we began renovations so we situated ourselves inside the house from hell as best as we could. While we started the process of gutting the house, we took baths in an old fashioned claw foot tub that sported creaky faucets and spouted brown water for a month, due to rust in the pipes. We knocked out every wall, which was easy since there wasn't much wiring in the place. Most of the plumbing was nonfunctional. We rented a 20-yard roll-off to put in the front yard for two months and filled it several times.

There were workers at the house every day ripping out walls, replacing plumbing, installing electrical outlets and wiring. The kids left for school one balmy spring morning in April and by the time they got home that afternoon, there was no kitchen left.

To console the girls and perhaps to punish myself, I decided to get two Border Collie pups we named Ginger and Lucy. When I brought them home, Angela's welcome wasn't quite as enthusiastic as I expected. "Are you out of your mind?" But the kids love the pups and that bought me a couple points. The dogs were added to our little menagerie, which included two cats we'd brought with us from Cincinnati. Another addition to our family was just what I needed between working here, there and everywhere.

Such was the double life I was living. I split my time between running Every Day Is Saturday and managing my rentals. I spent a few days in Bradford, a few in Springville, and twice a month I boarded a plane bound for a speaking engagement somewhere in the country. Three days a week I drove to Bradford and bought materials for my home renovation – carpet, paint, and cabinets –

then brought them home in my quest to restore the grand old lady to her former beauty.

The previous move back to Bradford just two years earlier ended up being a huge help because now I better understood the rental business and what I needed to do to make it work. And I wasn't intimidated by another move. I had a lot of different plates spinning in the air but I was passionate and confident about my ability to handle each and every one.

The end of summer came quickly. Our rundown house was almost out of rehab and our proximity to the rental properties allowed me to stay on top of managing them. Life was good until…

Angela woke me late one night with a frantic shove to my shoulder. "Honey!" she whispered. I rolled over and mumbled something about going back to sleep but she persisted. "Sam! There's a big bird flying through the house!"

It wasn't all that odd. A lot of the windows were cracked and we hadn't yet replaced them.

There was a lot of flapping and noisy commotion going on downstairs. I glanced at the clock next to the bed: three a.m. I rubbed the sleep out of my eyes and headed for the staircase landing.

Whoosh! A pair of webbed black wings came so close to my head, my hair whipped about in the breeze.

That was no bird – it was a bat!

I can handle a lot of things – but a bat? No way was I going to chase that thing down at three in the morning and try to avoid getting bit and contracting rabies. I grabbed a two by four and went back to bed, sleeping with one eye open the entire night.

As soon as the sun came up the next morning, I called the local animal control agency to come get the bat out of my belfry.

The animal control officer managed to get the bat cornered and into his big net without too much trauma. He grinned in triumph and showed me the proof of his success. He bagged the varmint and headed for my kitchen. "Now, then, we'll just put this baby in your fridge overnight until we get it tested for rabies. Right here next to the milk okay?"

Although I would have paid five times as much, I gave the guy a check for 25 dollars to take the bat away so he could test it for rabies at his leisure.

Later that morning I headed into town for breakfast at the local coffee shop. I saw several people I knew and I told them the story of our late night adventure. Apparently this was not a big deal. "You called Animal Control to get rid of it? Are you kidding me? We get three a week at our house!"

I asked one of them how the bat got into our house in the first place. The answer? "Old mineral siding. Ayup, that's right, Sam. That's what lettin' 'em in."

If the old siding, which was actually made out of asbestos and quite commonly used years ago, was the problem, then I needed to replace that stuff. I got right on it and within three weeks we had brand new siding on the house.

"That's all it took to get rid of the bats?" Angela asked, admiring the new look on the exterior of our home. I nodded, pleased that I would no longer have to worry about three a.m. bat calls.

By the time we were done renovating that house, it looked completely different than the dilapidated old thing we'd moved into months earlier. It now sported a brand new kitchen, refinished hardwood flooring, lush landscaping and a traditional, soft yellow color on the brand new siding.

We learned to enjoy living in the community of Springville. It was like living in Mayberry, RFD. The kids were thriving in school and they had lots of friends with whom to enjoy small town entertainment, like sledding and drinking hot chocolate in winter, and picking wildflowers in the summertime. It was a great environment for raising the girls; however, part of our hearts were still residing in Cincinnati, where we left our ultimate dream house.

The renters gave notice they were moving out in August of 2011 so I took the family back for Labor Day that year.

As soon as we walked through the front door, a wave of homesickness swept over us. I was more than ready to move back, but Angela put the brakes on my plans. "Let's take it slow and see how things go."

Of course that was the best course of action. Angela was right. She's right a lot – but don't ever tell her I said that.

Each remaining month of 2011 passed and the house in Cincinnati remained vacant. It was time for Angela and I to revisit our future plans. We waited until after the holidays were over, hired a babysitter, and went out to dinner to discuss what we wanted to do. It was just like that night in 2007 when we debated whether or not to move back to Bradford; once again we made a list of the pros and cons of living in each place.

Halfway through the list, we looked at each other and I voiced what both of us were thinking, "The hell with this! Let's just move back. That's where everyone wants to be. We're making this too much of an issue. We're trying to find reasons to stay here. Or…" A shard of an idea began to take

shape in my mind. "Why can't we have two houses
– one in Springville and one in Cincinnati? We
have options now – and that's what Every Day Is
Saturday is all about, after all. That's what I preach,
not having to decide between either/or options."

So we called the movers yet again and
they arrived at the old Victorian in Springville, in
January, 2012. One last time they loaded up all our
things and delivered them to the Crowley house
in Cincinnati.

There will always be a lot of armchair
quarterbacks in your life who think they know
what's best for you. Many of my friends and
family said they couldn't believe I'd moved my
family to Bradford, then back to Cincinnati, then
to Springville, and finally back to Cincinnati yet
again. "You're really fortunate they put up with
all that moving around. It must have been hell
on them."

"Not really," was my response. "Just ask the family." The kids stayed in contact with their friends via Skype and email; luckily these days it's not too difficult to maintain relationships over long distance, so it really wasn't that traumatic.

The thing those armchair quarterbacks fail to understand is that if I'd stayed in my corporate job, chances are I'd have moved my family seven or eight times over the same period. Hopefully I would have been relocated somewhere in the U.S. but that's never a given. If you are going to have a high level job, there will invariably be times when you have to make tough decisions, to perhaps suffer a bit in the short term in order to gain long term stability.

Angela and I looked at each move as an exciting journey, as a form of forced relocation that we decided upon together. Sure, it was a big undertaking, but it doesn't feel as forced when you're the one steering the boat.

Luckily, I've had the same property manager for a couple years and she's doing a great job. But every time we moved back to Bradford, I second guessed my decision to buy those rental properties. I soon realized the problem wasn't the rentals, it was my inability to find good people who could help me successfully manage them. Instead of asking for my problems to go away, I needed to ask myself to do a better job.

I'm only human and at times I've felt sorry for myself, even though I know that's a waste of time. It was particularly bad when I found out that Robert was stealing from me. I couldn't understand why someone would invoke God's name and then commit a blatant sin. But eventually I learned that I just need to quit trying to help everyone and learn from my mistakes. I've got to quit trying to be Robin Hood. Some people will never change for the better. A thief is a thief and is unlikely to change; they'll just steal more if you give them the opportunity and that's what I did – gave Robert an opportunity to rip me off.

Had I not moved back to Bradford – twice – and did all these crazy things, the speaking opportunities I've got now would never have materialized. Life works on the domino effect. Had I not been in a certain place at a certain time, I might never have met Les Brown and he might never have provided a video testimonial for me, which eventually led to other business opportunities. Even in the midst of loss and adversity, I put a smile on my face and acted as if I had all the answers. I'm not the only one to produce a series of motivational CDs, but I am the only one who can convey my message, in my way, and make it a big deal. People always want to be part of a big deal; they're ready to jump on your bandwagon if you just make it attractive enough.

All my life I've pushed the envelope – not necessarily to make money, but more to get a reaction from others. I want people to look at me and think, "What's Crowley got going on?" If everyone thinks you are doing things right, then you're not doing enough. Most people think I've got a screw or two loose and I have to admit they're probably right.

When I first started podcasting, my family nearly scheduled an intervention. "What are you doing, calling people 'Champion'? Have you lost your mind?" That made me realize I was on the right track because without that kind of feedback, I sure wasn't living life to the fullest.

Many people live in constant fear and doubt. They don't understand the greatness they have inside themselves. They become paralyzed by fear – the fear of failing or the fear of what someone else might think. Bill Cosby is noted for saying, "I don't know the key to success but the key to failure is trying to please everybody."

I used to be that person who always wanted to please others. But as an entrepreneur, that's not what makes you successful. When you work for yourself, it's not about pleasing others but about dialing in your personal moral compass. If others aren't in the same ZIP code as you, morally, don't worry about it. That doesn't mean you are offending someone in your target market demographic, it only means that you need to focus on reaching a different group. You can't control how your message is received, you can only speak it truthfully and from the heart. As soon as you stop trying to please everyone, you begin learning how to please yourself. Hey, kinda sounds like a song, doesn't it?

Yeah, I'm lucky I've got a wonderful family and support system. But it's about more than luck. I've designed my own life and I've got no one to blame but myself if things don't go smoothly. That's okay. I'm willing to accept that responsibility; entrepreneurialism sure beats being blown about by the winds of corporate change.

Who knows where I'll end up next? All I know is I'm comfortable right here, right now. I know that something will eventually come along to change things but I know it will happen for a reason.

What about you – where are you headed? If it's to a destination not of your own choosing, then now is the time to make a change. Maybe it's time to re-enter the woods, bears be damned!

Chapter Sixteen:

Who Do You Think You Are?

More than anything else, it's important to have an identity of which you can be proud, not just for some of the time but all of the time. All the success in the world means nothing if you can't look at yourself in the mirror each day and like what you see.

Over the years I've had a lot of people ask me who I think I am. At a young age, I was cocky enough to think I knew the answer to that question. It wasn't until recently, however, that I really came to terms with not only my true self, but what my definition of success is really all about. Going through all those moves between Cincinnati and Bradford taught me that success without fulfillment is failure. And fulfillment is all about liking that face in the mirror, knowing you've done your best to help others.

When I look back at my childhood and everything I experienced over the course of my life, it only seems natural that fulfillment would become an integral part of success in my mind. Yes, it's been a long, strange journey– from poverty and happiness in a small town, to success and wealth in the big city, and finally a return home to both happiness and a reaffirmation of my values. But without going through that journey, I wouldn't be able to appreciate those simple joys I first encountered during my childhood – and they are priceless.

It all started in Bradford, of course. I always had an attitude and I always knew I had to do things my own way and that was no secret to my friends and family. I never did anything to please others and that's a fact perhaps best represented by my stint as student council president in high school.

There were 900 kids in my high school and about a third of them in my graduating class. I had a lot of friends and I knew pretty much everybody but I didn't really expect to win the student council president race. That election was really just a popularity contest but still... Imagine my surprise when I won by a landslide!

Now what? My first official act was to appoint my buddy Mike A. (yeah, my later drinking buddy) vice president. Over the course of our senior year, Mike and I just did what we wanted to do, which was, basically, nothing. To call us figureheads of the student government would be an injustice to figureheads everywhere. It was the worst student government in the history of the school.

But the position came with some perks. I was interviewed for an article in the student newspaper titled, "Who Is Sam Crowley?" What 17-year-old kid doesn't want to see his name in the newspaper? The article came out a few weeks after the interview. It included such hard-hitting questions as "What is one of your biggest life goals?" My answer? "To make $100,000 by the time I'm thirty." What a joke! I might as well have made the figure a billion dollars for all the likelihood that would happen!

I got flak over this for a long time, both in school and out. My gym teacher brought it up that day in class. "You think you can make a $1,000,000 by the time you're 30-years-old?" *Huh?* "It's right here in the paper." The reporter had added an extra zero. Now I really appeared to be full of myself!

My own family ribbed me about the article, too. "Hmm, Sam. Who are you? Do we even know who you are?"

I should have expected it. Very few people say what they really think. I just blurt out whatever is on my mind. Yeah, I did want to make $1,000,000! There wasn't a kid in my high school who didn't dream of doing the same, but they were too afraid to say so because they didn't want to deal with the repercussions. They didn't have any confidence and that really highlighted the difference between them and me. I didn't have anything to lose and I wasn't worried about looking silly. *Who did I think I was?* Sam…just Sam. But that was enough.

Most of the time shy people don't speak up because they have a fear of offending others. But that needs to be turned back around to the person receiving the message; it's up to them how they process it, positively or negatively.

During my adolescence, I heard a lot of things that were less than flattering. But I couldn't internalize them – I just had to put those comments into context. If Mom had been drinking, I had to process her words and decide if it was really Mom – or the alcohol – talking.

I developed a really thick skin that prevented me from crying in front of my classmates, and later my own children. I didn't even realize until my daughters told me recently that they've never seen me get emotional. My mom was the same way; she seldom broke down during all those difficult times in my childhood. I want to be more sensitive but honestly, there's not a lot that gets to me, especially when I'm out in public or part of a group. I've learned to internalize everything and process it before responding at a later date, because of my childhood – growing up with a father, dealing with an alcoholic mother, speaking with a stutter. I've never wanted to be a weak person or be viewed as someone who is flawed. All things should be processed at the right time and because I know how to do it, I'm not afraid of saying or doing anything.

On the last day of my senior year in high school, the administration held an assembly to swear in the new president. The assistant principal stood up in front of all the students and gave a speech. "We're going to bring student government back to Bradford High School! It will no longer be a joke. We welcome in the new president, hoping he doesn't duplicate what we just went through over the past year." Yeah, he was that sorry to see me go.

Anytime you put yourself out there you become a target. You will get ribbed. You will push people's buttons and shake them up a bit. It's like moving someone else's cheese – when you become that person whom others are talking about, it shows you have confidence, and highlights other people's failures.

I'm still putting myself out there and making people think. And because of that, I get a lot of questions, such as, "Who do you think you are, making every day a Saturday?"

When you shake people up, they get uncomfortable – but they also start to think,

"If Sam can do it, I can do it, too." Controversy highlights my own confidence while helping to empower others. The great speaker and author Jim Rohn once said, "Discipline weighs ounces while regret weighs tons." As long as you have enough discipline to say crazy things and take action, you own your goals.

No one from my high school was going to follow up with me at the age of 30 and find out whether or not I'd made my $1,000,000. But it was still important for me to say what I wanted because that helps me to hold myself accountable. Years later I was the one who asked myself, "How's that website working? Are you speaking yet? You said you would be on stages all around the world – why haven't you done it?"

I had a big strike against me when I started Every Day Is Saturday because everyone knew I'd filed bankruptcy. It seemed impossible to turn that around 180 degrees into a multi-million dollar business, but I did. Yet, when success happened, all those naysayers never did come back and tell me, "Congratulations!" The snipers who mocked and ridiculed me were no longer around.

Understand right now that you will take flak for pursuing your dreams, but very rarely will you get the opportunity to see all those doubters eat crow later.

That interview in the student newspaper all those long years ago was just the start of many controversial, in-your-face type comments I would make – never to harm anyone else or target any individual or group to bring them down – but to lift myself up, to challenge myself. It's not a challenge to respond to others who tell me what I can't do. It is a challenge to overcome my own fears and live up to my own standards. Once I say something, anything, I own it.

By the time I was 30-years-old, I *was* making $100,000. I think that subconsciously I owned that goal and I made it happen, all because of that interview in high school. That goal became reality. I made a point to bring it up at class reunions. "Remember how you ribbed me about my dream of making $100,000? I actually did that!"

That was all well and good but I got a little too caught up in the money and fame aspect of my career. So that first time I lost my property manager and had to move back to Bradford, a part of me was anxious to see how successful I could be with my rentals, but there was another part of me that dreaded relocating. I'd been in the corporate world so long I couldn't imagine going back to life in a small town where people scrape by without a lot of money or material possessions. Even though I was no longer wearing a suit and tie every day or working out of that plush corner office, I still had that CEO mindset. I was still in that world where if I just worked harder than anyone else, I could be more successful.

And then I had to become a maintenance man! I had to return to that small town where I'd grown up and deal with tenants who were too poor to own their own homes, people in blue collar jobs who took public transportation to work each day. I was subconsciously looking down my nose at them before I'd even met them in person. "What are you going to do my units?" was how I viewed them…at first.

I had about 40 tenants or so. And just like any other group of people with whom you must deal, such as your employees or clients, 10 percent of them would cause 90 percent of the problems. Those were the people who would move out in the middle of the night after kicking holes in the walls and owing back rent. But 90 percent of them were just some really nice folks. They weren't bad people; they didn't have a lot of money or a nice car but they didn't let that lack of "things" get in the way of their fulfillment. Many of them were adults who just couldn't afford their own home mixed in with a handful of students who lived on strict budgets.

As I spent those months in Bradford collecting rent and shoveling sidewalks, I learned their stories. Many of them would invite me into their homes to enjoy a cup of hot chocolate, or cookies, or just a chat about life, family, grandkids or whatever else was on their minds. It became more than just a landlord-tenant relationship, these people became respected friends.

It didn't take me long to become embarrassed about how I'd prejudged them just because of their living circumstances. I assumed they were missing out on the best life had to offer. But I quickly realized it wasn't those go-getters I'd once known in the corporate office, the ones living in penthouses and driving fancy cars, who were fulfilled. The corporate environment is where sell outs go to live. Those people who will sell their soul to get what they truly desire – a promotion, social acceptance, job security – they belong in the rat race, spinning their wheels in a little cubicle.

My tenants were all snuggled into one- or two-bedroom apartments. But they're the ones who had things figured out. They weren't running from anything and they knew they didn't need worldly possessions to be happy. They showed me that people are not content because they are wealthy, they are wealthy because they are content. These people focused on particular hobbies and interests that brought them joy and fulfillment; not things that required a lot of money.

That's a tough lesson to learn, to really integrate into your own life.

One of my tenants in particular, a grandmother named Terrie who rented a one-bedroom apartment from me, helped to nudge me down the road to true fulfillment. Terrie and I always chatted as I performed routine maintenance in her building. Often I spent an hour or more talking with her, but I didn't mind at all. She was wise, and kind, and just downright nice.

The first month I was back in Bradford, Terrie's stove quit working. I took a look at it and shook my head. She'd been renting the same apartment for some 17 years and the stove was about that old. It was well-used, to put it nicely.

"Do you think you could get me a new stove?" Terrie asked me one day that fall. "I'm a baker and I love making things for my grandkids. I'd like to bake them some cookies and brownies."

While my biggest focus was Every Day Is Saturday and internet marketing and podcasting, this lovely old woman's focus was baking for her family over the holidays. That was the one thing that would make her happy – a new stove for baking goodies.

That same day I went to Sears and bought Terrie a brand new stove. It wasn't anything special, just a regular model with a shiny new finish and a ten-year warranty, but to Terrie it was like getting a Rolls Royce. I watched that stove being delivered to her home, and seeing the look of sheer joy on her face made a tremendous impact on me. It made me realize how unimportant it is to have flashy and expensive "stuff" just to impress others.

Watching Terrie also reminded me of my own experience in Bradford when I was growing up. My family didn't have a lot of money or nice cars but we sure did make great holiday memories. In fact, I lived vicariously through Terrie and her delight in Thanksgiving and Christmas that year, and it brought me back full circle to my roots. As the youngest of eight kids growing up in Bradford, I'd actually lived only one block away from Terrie's apartment. I could almost see myself, as a kid, being welcomed into her apartment to the smell of pumpkin pie and the warmth of her hug.

I began to question my priorities. I had a beautiful wife, a wonderful family, and good health…what more did I need? I realized that if I hadn't taken that leap of faith and moved back to Bradford, I would have escaped the hard work of becoming a hands-on landlord and property manager. Yet…I'm glad I didn't escape it. I became excited, reborn, and fulfilled in this small town that looks like a scene straight out of a Norman Rockwell painting. Springville was like that, too, a place where my small family grew closer, a place to stop and enjoy Christmas lights in the midst of a falling snow, or a field of brightly hued flowers beneath a wash of brilliant, summer sunlight.

Someday I'll go back again to that small town environment. That's where I'll die – in a place where I enjoy simple moments with my family; playing games, swimming in a public pool, and sledding in the snow. I guess what they say is true: You can take the boy out of the small town, but you can't take the small town out of the boy.

No matter how much knowledge and experience and things you acquire, you will always go back to the person you really are, deep down inside. When I started Every Day Is Saturday, I did it because I wanted to focus on being a dad; it had nothing to do with money. But as I began earning a comfortable income and getting contracted for huge speaking gigs, my entrepreneurial world began to mirror that corporate world I'd left behind. All of a sudden I was surrounded once again by people with immense wealth, driving imported sports cars and living in penthouses. It took a trip back to Bradford, PA to make me realize that these people weren't content. You can spend your whole life searching for fulfillment and happiness, but the best things in life really are free.

Over the holiday season in 2010 I got a call that Terrie had passed away from cancer. My first thought was that she would have been sad not to have used her stove that year to bake sweet treats for her grandkids.

I attended the viewing and made a point of talking to Terrie's children and grandchildren, telling them how much she had loved them all. It was the same funeral home where the town had paid their last respects to my mother; in fact Terrie's casket was displayed in the exact same room. And just like my mom, the entire town attended this viewing, too.

As I gazed down at Terrie's sweet, kind face, a wave of deep emotion swept over me. I remembered buying her that stove and I was never more proud of any other thing I'd done in my life. She may not have had a mansion with an ocean view, but she did have a knack for experiencing Saturday, every day she spent baking snicker doodles in that oven.

Life, of course, is finite and that limited amount of time on earth is precious. I can't lose sight of who I really am. I may be a worldwide motivational speaker but my heart and soul are – and always will be – from Bradford. I can only hope that someday I have the same impact on others as my mom and Terrie did. The kind of impact that has nothing to do with money and everything to do with who you really are – the real face you see staring back from the mirror.

The rules about life I first learned in Bradford, and then relearned during my time as landlord and maintenance man, are still with me each and every day. The more money I've made, the more I've given back to help others. It's not about who has the most toys at the end of life, it's about who spent the most time with their family and enjoyed the best health, both mentally and physically. I used to live in the corporate world of sellouts once, but now in the entrepreneurial world,

I get to choose with whom to surround myself. I get to decide what's best for me and my family, and it feels really, really good to choose the high road.

Life has been one big journey with no end in sight. As I write this book, I haven't even begun to do everything I want. At this point, I'm just getting out of the harbor, putting my boat in motion.

At many moments along my journey to fulfillment things weren't so good and my vision wasn't quite so clear. But now…now, I'm content being who I am: a loose cannon, someone who rejoices in doing the wrong things, knowing I can make mistakes but continuing to be happy with who I am. I learn from my mistakes instead of punishing myself. When I lay my head down on the pillow each night, I'm comfortable with my own uniqueness – and my own flaws.

Moving forward, understand that your Saturday is whatever you want it to be. It's a self-fulfilling prophecy of your own design. Just like

Terrie, your Saturday can be baking cookies every day or caring for family members if that's what makes you happy. It's not about being a sellout. It's not about going to a job you hate every day just because the money's good.

It's not easy to become your own boss. You will be uncomfortable. You will lose a lot of the people in your life right now. As an entrepreneur, you will be thrown into a pool and expected to swim with the sharks. You must allow people to mouth off to you – but you must also understand what's in their hearts. Take the time to process from where the words are coming; it could be that someone is battling an addiction, a terminal disease, or unemployment. There's always more to the situation than what someone shows on the surface.

So...take control and move forward! You cannot steer a ship that is still sitting in the harbor. At some point you have to leave the safety of the marina and crash into big waves and maybe get a little seasick.

Your Saturday can be designed right here and right now without any money. All you need is a big dream whose core is about fulfillment and adding value to the lives of others.

You'll know when you've arrived at a year full of Saturdays. The test is to take a moment each day and look at the clock. If you can say, "I can't believe I've got to stop doing what I'm doing right now because I love it so much" then you've passed the test – it is, indeed, Saturday!

Are you ready to start your own journey? Just who do you think you are? How will you make tomorrow the first day of a life full of Saturdays, Champion?

END NOTES

If you'd like to connect with Sam Crowley or for media inquires and speaker requests, please send an email to Sam@EveryDayIsSaturday.com.

Be sure to plug into Every Day Is Saturday message online, too. You can access fresh new content and loads of motivational messages by visiting www.EveryDayIsSaturday.com.

If you liked this book, please take a moment to let us know by adding a review on www.Amazon.com.

Thank you for reading and learning how to turn every day of your life into Saturday!

Made in the USA
San Bernardino, CA
10 December 2012